D1500426

Communion with the Saints, A Family Preparation Program for First Communion and Beyond in the Spirit of St. Therese

Janet P. McKenzie, OCDS

A RACE for Heaven Product

Biblio Resource Publications, Inc.
Bessemer, Michigan

ISBN 978-1-934185-18-6

Published by
Biblio Resource Publications, Inc.
108½ South Moore Street
Bessemer, MI 49911
www.BiblioResourcePublications.com
info@BiblioResource.com

A **R**ead **A**loud **C**urriculum **E**nrichment Product
www.RACEforHeaven.com

Cover photo © kryczka_d - Fotolia.com
Cover flower petals © Paul Maguire - Fotolia.com

Printed in the United States of America

Dedication

On the feast of her glorious Assumption 2007, this program is dedicated to the Most Blessed Virgin Mary in thanksgiving for her constant intercession and for the model of fervent prayer that she has given us: "And Mary kept all these things, reflecting on them in her heart." (Luke 2:19)

Our Lady of Mount Carmel, pray for us!

Communion with the Saints, A Family Preparation Program for First Communion and Beyond in the Spirit of St. Therese

Table of Contents

Communion with the Saints, A Family Preparation Program for First Communion and Beyond in the Spirit of St. Therese

General Instructions

Introduction

St. Therese of the Child Jesus began her specific preparation for Holy Communion on Saturday, March 1, 1884, and received this sacrament on Thursday, May 8, 1884—a period that covers sixty-nine days or almost ten weeks. [Note that the original date set for Therese's First Holy Communion, May 29, was later changed to May 8.] This program is designed to begin on a Monday, sixty-nine days before the Sunday on which the reception of First Holy Communion would occur. (However, each day is numbered for the convenience of those who receive the sacrament on a day other than a Sunday.)

During her sixty-nine day preparation period, St. Therese was carefully instructed by her sister Pauline, a Carmelite nun known as Sr. Agnes of Jesus, who prepared a "copybook" with prayers, pious thoughts, and the practice of virtue through the image of the cultivation of various flowers. The following letter from Sr. Agnes of Jesus to Therese was written in February 1884:

> This morning, I promised Marie I'd give you the little copybook for the beginning of March. I'm working on it all the time. I hope my Benjamin will work very hard, too, in order to cultivate her little garden. To plant flowers in this garden which are just as beautiful as those in the little copybook, she must not allow one single weed in it.
>
> Oh! when I think that in three months' time Jesus will come to rest in this little child's heart, in my Thérésita's heart!
>
> You must, darling, spare yourself nothing to make your soul a little heaven where the Child Jesus will want to dwell forever!
>
> Ah! may this gentle Child already be the King, the love of your heart. What is there on earth more delightful than Jesus? Jesus in His cradle, Jesus in Thérésita's heart on May 29 . . . sleeping among flowers! (John Clarke, translator, *General Correspondence Volume 1,* page 185)

Therese's sister Marie also instructed Therese in the doctrines of the faith and especially in the sanctity of the Sacrament of Holy Eucharist. This program too relies upon the instruction and interaction of various family members.

Program Outline

Communion with the Saints, A Family Preparation Program for First Communion and Beyond in the Spirit of St. Therese is a program of preparation for and appreciation of the Sacrament of Holy Communion. It can be used to aid in preparing a family member to receive the Sacrament of Holy Eucharist for the first time, or it can serve as a second beginning for those who may have lost fervor for this sacrament. If this program is used with a first communicant, be sure to include the weekend reading, journal entries, and readings. When the program is used only with those who are already receiving this sacrament, the weekend readings and projects may be eliminated if desired. All of the readings from the main texts of this program are read and reviewed during the weekdays.

The program has several components: a study guide for the four main texts with corresponding answer keys, additional daily readings for older siblings, weekend family projects, journal entries, and optional catechism lessons. These components—as well as the books necessary for each component—are described and outlined below.

The following books are <u>required</u> to complete the *Communion with the Saints* program:

📖 Three Mary Fabyan Windeatt books: *The Little Flower, The Story of St. Therese of the Child Jesus; The Children of Fatima and Our Lady's Message to the World* and *The Patron Saint of First Communicants, The Story of Blessed Imelda Lambertini*

📖 Mother Mary Loyola's *King of the Golden City, An Allegory for Children* (any edition of the book or one of the many audio editions available)

📖 *The Story of a Soul, The Autobiography of St. Therese of Lisieux* (for students grade 7 and beyond—see page v below for more information)

📖 Catholic Bible for the study of Scripture

<u>Optional</u> materials include the following:

✟ *My First Communion Journal in Imitation of St. Therese, The Little Flower* <u>OR</u> *My First Communion Journal in Imitation of St. Paul: Putting on the Armor of God*

✟ For first communicants, either the Faith and Life second grade religion book, *Jesus Our Life,* or *The New Saint Joseph First Communion Catechism*

✟ For siblings grades 3-5, *The New Saint Joseph Baltimore Catechism, Book No. 1;* and for siblings grades 6-8, *The New Saint Joseph Baltimore Catechism, Book No. 2*

✟ Either the *Catechism of the Catholic Church,* or *Compendium of the Catechism of the Catholic Church* for students beyond eighth grade (See "Optional Catechism Lessons" below for more specific instructions.)

✟ *Eucharist Miracles* by Joan Carroll Cruz or *This Is My Body, This Is My Blood: Miracles of the Eucharist* by Bob and Penny Lord (Either of these books may be used as a religion text for older siblings who already have a solid grasp of the catechism.)

✟ *The Story of a Family, The Home of the Little Flower (St. Thérèse of Lisieux)* by Father Stéphane-Joseph Piat (for parents—see page v below for more information)

Study Guide

The *Communion with the Saints* study guide contains a chapter-by-chapter review of four books in the following order:

1. *The Little Flower, The Story of St. Therese of the Child Jesus* by Mary Fabyan Windeatt—to reveal the foundation of God's love for us and to encourage a desire for holiness
2. *The Children of Fatima and Our Lady's Message to the World* by Mary Fabyan Windeatt—to show the sinfulness of our world and the need to avoid sin
3. *The Patron Saint of First Communicants, The Story of Blessed Imelda Lambertini* by Mary Fabyan Windeatt—to inspire devotion to the Holy Eucharist
4. Mother Mary Loyola's *The King of the Golden City Study Edition* by Janet McKenzie—to illustrate Jesus' Presence as the source of grace necessary to live a holy life

In each of these books, one or more chapters are to be read aloud each day as outlined in the study guide. After the oral reading, complete the additional exercises together as a family. As the format for the Windeatt biographies and *The King of the Golden City* are somewhat different, they will be reviewed separately.

Format for the Windeatt Biographies

Comprehension Questions/Narration Prompts

Several questions are provided for each chapter; answers are provided in the answer key. These questions can be used in a variety of ways:

- If read aloud before the reading of the chapter, they can serve as a cue to the important content of each chapter.
- After reading the chapter, they can serve as a test of the listeners' comprehension.
- Use them as prompts when the listeners narrate the chapter after its oral reading.

Discussion Topics

These topics may be discussed together orally to provide an expansion of the material contained in each chapter, and to inspire spiritual family conversation.

Growing in Holiness

Each day a practical application of at least one religious lesson is provided. The importance of this part of the program cannot be overemphasized. Remember that it is not enough to know of God—as through the catechism and the Bible. We must actually know and experience God Himself. Through prayer, sacrifice, and a conversion of our minds and hearts, we may come to know and imitate Him more each day.

Optional Catechism Lessons

These lessons may be utilized for those who wish to incorporate the study of the doctrines of the Church into their preparation program. For a child who is preparing to receive his/her First Holy Communion, choose either the Faith and Life second grade religion book, *Jesus Our Life,* or *The New Saint Joseph First Communion Catechism* as the religious text. By following the plan outlined for each chapter, either of these catechisms will be completed by the end of the program.

Children in grades 3 through 8 should follow the outline for *The New Saint Joseph Baltimore Catechism, Book No. 1* or *Book No. 2*, depending on the ages of the student. Both of these texts will be covered in their entirety by the end of the sixty-nine days.

High-school students should use the *Catechism of the Catholic Church* or the *Compendium* as their religious text. The references for the more concise *Compendium* appear in parentheses after the *CCC* citations. Older siblings can read aloud—and then discuss—the stated text paragraphs with an adult.

Older siblings who already know their doctrine well may prefer to use one of the following books as a religious text: *Eucharist Miracles* by Joan Carroll Cruz, or *This Is My Body, This Is My Blood: Miracles of the Eucharist* by Bob and Penny Lord.

Format for The King of the Golden City

The format for this section is the same for both the "Discussion Topics" and the "Growing in Holiness" sections. Other exercises are outlined below. (Although these activities are included in *The King of the Golden City Study Edition*, they are also included here for those who own a different edition of the book or for those who wish to use the audio version of this book.)

Narration

Instead of answering comprehension questions, students are asked to narrate each day's oral reading. Siblings— beginning with the youngest—should be asked to narrate or tell back the story after the oral reading. Older family members should then add further details to the first narration. Especially at first, it may be easier to pause between chapters to narrate rather than wait until both chapters of the daily lesson have been read.

Parallel Figures Chart

After the day's reading and narration are complete, characters, objects, and events should be entered onto a large chart. This chart, constructed of either notebook paper or a large sheet of poster board, will list—from the beginning of the book until the end—important characters, objects, and events in one column and what each of these symbolizes, or parallels, in the next column. Be open to characters or objects symbolizing more than one thing. Perhaps it may seem to parallel one thing but as more information is gathered, it more likely parallels something different. This project should be completed as a family project. Characters, objects, and events to be deciphered are listed for each chapter, although an attentive listener will find more. Some possible parallels for each character, object and event are included in the answer key.

Searching Scripture

Passages from Holy Scripture are selected for each chapter of *The King of the Golden City*. Encourage older siblings to make a connection between the biblical citations and the text within each chapter. Help them relate God's Word to life's events and decisions.

Carmelite Connections

For those interested in deepening their prayer life, this section provides quotations from several Carmelite saints including St. Teresa of Avila, St. John of the Cross, and St. Therese of the Child Jesus. These quotations provide helpful comments on the transformation of the little maid as she deepens her friendship with the King and progresses in heroic virtue and spiritual perfection. Older siblings and adults can profit from the teachings of the Carmelite saints regarding our relationship with God as well as the stages and methods of deep Carmelite prayer. Allow these saints to assist you in understanding God's love and desire for us, the obstacles to an intimate relationship with Him, and how to make true progress toward perfect union with our Lord and King.

Optional Catechism Lessons

For first communicants, the review of the catechism continues in the same format as done in prior weeks. However, with the completion of the three biographies, older siblings using either *Book No. 1* or *Book No. 2* of *The New Saint Joseph Baltimore Catechism* will have completed their catechism review. Now comes the time to apply their catechetical knowledge. Several articles of doctrine or vocabulary words from the catechism are listed for each chapter. Siblings should define these words or phrases using, if necessary, the "Dictionary and Index" section found at the back of the catechism. Additionally, the index lists the question number where the word/phrase can be located; the questions of the catechism should be reviewed and studied as necessary. All words and phrases can be located in both *The New Saint Joseph Baltimore Catechism, Book No. 1* and *Book No. 2* unless otherwise noted.

Encourage the students to think through the reason why each word/phrase is included for each chapter. Have them attempt to find a passage in *The King of the Golden City* that corresponds to the specific word or phrase cited. This allows them to see how the Faith as presented in the catechism is enacted in daily life.

Additional Daily 7

Parents are encouraged to read *The Story of a Family, The Home of The Little Flower (St. Thérèse of Lisieux)* by Fr. Stéphane-Joseph Piat in conjunction with this program. This book provides much inspiration regarding the home life and spiritual habits of the Martin family. As this book is rather lengthy (over 400 pages), a reading schedule of ten or so pages per day has been included with each day's lessons. Weekends are used to catch up on any reading not completed during the week.

Older students are asked to read *The Story of a Soul, The Autobiography of St. Therese of Lisieux* in conjunction with the Windeatt biography of St. Therese. This schedule is included in the study guide. Thereafter, the short meditational readings for this age group are contained in the "Reading Schedule for High School and Middle School Students" beginning on page 77 below. Be sure to read the two abridged papal encyclicals presented on pages 93-101.

If desired, the readings outlined in the "Reading Schedule" may be replaced with readings from either *Eucharist Miracles* by Joan Carroll Cruz or *This Is My Body, This Is My Blood: Miracles of the Eucharist* by Bob and Penny Lord. Parents too will benefit from these books.

Weekend Projects

The study guide provides readings and exercises—both oral and written—for all the weekdays of the sixty-nine days of the *Communion with the Saints* program. Some short meditational readings for older siblings are also provided for the weekend. The "Weekend Projects" section of this program provides a variety of activities ranging from field trips, craft projects, family discussions, parish involvement, family apostolates, and the establishment of family traditions. Far more activities are suggested than a family will be able to complete within the time frame of this program. Prayerfully choose those activities that best match your family's needs and interests. (Perhaps call a family meeting.)

Review the suggested projects well in advance in order to lay out a possible project schedule for the first nine weekends of the program. To aid in scheduling, a summary list of all projects is included on page 112. Use this list to record completed projects and review upcoming projects. Try to complete at least one activity each weekend. Some projects are ongoing in nature, and some will be difficult to complete within one weekend. Plan accordingly.

Journal

The following letter was written by Sr. Agnes of Jesus, St. Therese's sister Pauline, from the Carmelite convent to Therese on February 28, 1884:

> I don't know if it's you who will come tomorrow morning to get this short note. In any case, I'm informing you about the famous copybook for this evening. When I think that my Thérérsita will begin her great preparation on Saturday morning! Only two months and a half and little Jesus will come down for the first time into her heart! Oh! how necessary it is to use these two months and a half well! How much work to do and how many flowers to sow in so little time! But, my dear, look at nature. It is beginning to repair its dress almost on the same day as yourself. We already see buds on the trees in gardens, and very soon the flowers will appear. Certainly during the month of May everything will charm the eyes. Well, what nature is doing just to give joy to our eyes, will you not do also, Thérérsita of the Child Jesus, to receive and give joy to the beloved little Child at His first awakening in your heart?
>
> However, I hear your answer, and I feel it's almost useless to encourage you when one possesses a good little heart like yours, my darling!
>
> I feel that from a distance Jesus Himself is inviting and encouraging His little sister to work for Him, and so what are your poor Agnes' incentives compared to little Jesus' gentle words?
>
> Adieu, Thérérsita. If your little garden is in bloom, if all is ready when the great day arrives, believe that Jesus will not come with empty hands! Ah! If you only knew the delightful treasures hidden in this little Host of a well-prepared First Communion! Your Agnes (Clarke, *General Correspondence Vol. 1,* pages 187-88)

The "famous copybook" to which Sr. Agnes refers is described in the footnote for the preceding letter as follows: ". . . one page for each day. Each page was decorated with a border, rays in each of the corners, the date in Gothic illumination, the name of a flower and a short invocation which the scent of the flower symbolized; it was all done in black and red ink. The flyleaf was particularly well done. Prayers to the Child Jesus, the Blessed Virgin, St. Joseph, the guardian angel preface each of the . . . months. Preparation was to begin on March 1." (As Therese received her first Holy Communion on Thursday, May 8, 1884, her preparation period was sixty-nine days.)

In another letter to Therese (February 29, 1884), Sr. Agnes again refers to the copybook with its cover of blue velvet, embroidered with the initials "T M" in white. (John Clarke, translator, *General Correspondence Volume 1*, pages 189-90)

Celine too had a copybook similar to the one Sr. Agnes prepared for Therese: ". . . Pauline prepared Celine for her First Communion. She put together for her, as she later did for Therese, a little book where, under the symbols of flowers, the little girl could record her sacrifices and her pious thoughts." (Fr. Stéphane-Joseph Piat, *The Story of a Family, The Home of St. Thérèse of Lisieux*, page 19)

Format for My First Communion Journal

Two Separate Themes

Two separate themes are presented in the journals: *My First Communion Journal in Imitation of St. Therese, the Little Flower* presents a <u>floral theme</u> (in imitation of St. Therese's copybook) and *My First Communion Journal in Imitation of St. Paul: Putting on the Armor of God* presents a <u>battle theme</u>, for those less inclined toward the study of flowers.

The floral theme is appropriate for a number of reasons. First, as noted above, St. Therese herself was given instruction for her First Holy Communion with this theme. Secondly, St. Therese is known as "The Little Flower." In her autobiography *The Story of a Soul*, St. Therese sets the title of the manuscript as the "Springtime Story of a Little White Flower." She uses the title of "Little Flower" when referring to herself twenty-four times within this manuscript. This title derives from several sources: When Therese approached her father with her desire to enter Carmel, he responded by plucking a small white flower (lily of the valley) from the garden, explaining to her that care with which God had preserved and cared for that flower. She compares His care for the little flower with the care He has bestowed upon His little Therese. (Therese kept this flower in her copy of *The Imitation of Christ*.) Upon receiving permission from her uncle to enter Carmel, he too used this metaphor, telling her that she was a little white flower God wanted to gather. The Vietnamese martyr St. Theophane Venard, who was a great hero to Therese, was also fond of the image of a spring flower. This image of a small white flower suited the spirituality of Therese and her "Little Way." Within the first pages of the story of her life, Therese uses the image of the rose versus that of the wildflower to illustrate her "Little Way," for if all creation esteemed to be great as roses, much would be lost. Therese of Lisieux teaches us that the simplicity and littleness of a soul in union with the will of God enriches and beautifies the Kingdom of God.

In addition to *My First Communion Journal in Imitation of St. Therese, The Little Flower* imitating the study of virtues as associated with flowers, it also imitates the preparation of St. Therese for First Holy Communion by encouraging sacrifice, a focus on things above, and a growth in humility. St. Therese's "copybook" contained several short prayers (or aspirations) to be prayed many times daily and space to note the small sacrifices made each day to please Jesus. She kept track of how many times she raised her heart to Jesus and how many sacrifices she made daily by counting them on her "sacrifice beads" (a small chaplet of moveable beads) and noting them daily in her book. This journal includes these prayers and has space for recording the number of times the prayers are recited as well as space to note the number of sacrifices (or mortifications) made each day.

The alternative battle theme, as presented in *My First Communion Journal in Imitation of St. Paul: Putting on the Armor of God,* centers on our earthly life as a battle. This journal also contains the simple prayers used by St. Therese (along with several additional ones) as well as space for noting the number of times recited each day and the number of sacrifices made. However, rather than imitating the virtues the flowers present to us, we are encouraged to cultivate virtuous habits by putting on God's armor (Ephesians 6:10-17) as we battle through our earthly life in our fight for eternal glory.

Holy Scripture
St. Therese's knowledge and love of Holy Scripture is evident in her writings. Quotations from both the Old and New Testament permeate her writings; her autobiography, *The Story of a Soul,* contains over 150 scriptural references. To encourage this knowledge and love of Scripture, each journal contains numerous biblical passages suitable for memorization.

Study of the Mass

The matching activity found on pages 75-76 helps to familiarize the students with the scriptural basis for the words used in the Mass. Answers for this exercise are provided in the answer key. As this is not a comprehensive list, challenge them to find others.

However, other than this one matching worksheet and the overviews provided in the catechisms, the *Communion with the Saints* program does not contain much study of the Mass. Many resources are available from various Catholic vendors that include a more in-depth study. For your convenience, several of these are listed below.

Miniature Mass Kit for Children contains a chalice, paten, censer, bell, snuffer, crucifix, candles, cruets, finger bowl, sanctuary light, incense/charcoal, and directions for making altar cloths such as the finger towel, purificator, pall, and corporal. The lesson booklet has directions for constructing a wooden altar and tray. (See Our Father's House at OurFathersHouse.biz.)

This Is My Body by Mark P. Shea is a study on the True Presence, which relies on Scripture and Tradition. Julia Fogassy of Our Father's House also provides a five-week study guide for this book for middle school ages and above.

The Mass Explained to Children by Maria Montessori was originally published in 1932. This delightful book explains many aspects of the Mass: its meaning, what is necessary for the Mass, an introduction to the Mass, the Mass of the Catechumens, and the Mass of the Faithful. It also contains an easy-to-read commentary on the Latin Mass with most parts applicable to the Novus Ordo Mass as well. It has been recently republished by Roman Catholic Books.

The Essence of the Mass published by Catholic Heritage Curricula contains explanations of the Mass for children as well as more in-depth meditations and commentaries for older children and adults.

Discovering the Treasures of the Mass: 28 Puzzles that Teach Its Rites and Rituals by Lynne Sterritt and published by Twenty-Third Publications for high school and middle school students is full of information about the action and prayers of the Mass in a fun format.

A Biblical Walk through the Mass: Understanding What We Say and do in the Liturgy is written by Edward Sri and published by Ascension Press. Based on the 2011 revised translation of the Mass, this book explores the biblical roots of the actions and words we use in the Mass and relates the long-standing tradition of the Mass.

Living Books on the Mass:

The Weight of a Mass, A Tale of Faith by Josehpine Nobisso—a picture book based upon a true story which enhances the appreciation of the Mass for all ages. This beautifully written and illustrated book emphasizes the depth and richness of the Holy Sacrifice of the Mass in a simple tale that will be enjoyed by all ages.

Outlaws of Ravenhurst Study Edition by Sister M. Imelda Wallace and Janet P. McKenzie—a novel originally written in 1950 and republished by Neumann Press that tells the story of the Catholic persecutions of seventeenth-century Scotland where participating in Mass meant death. This excellent family read-aloud choice is an exciting tale that will not soon be forgotten.

Conclusion

Many suggestions for the use of this program are included above. It is important to remember that they are only suggestions. It is very easy to get absorbed into a program as established by someone else and forget the importance of tailoring the program to fit your family's—and each specific child's—current needs. It is a poor program that will not lend itself to adaptation. Feel free—in fact please do—adjust this program to fit your particular needs. Do only those activities that you deem necessary and fruitful; add or substitute other materials if you feel they are more useful than the material suggested.

Only one rule applies to the use of this program: Every day each family member must do some spiritual reading—either orally or silently—and must spend some time in silent meditation in front of a crucifix or before the tabernacle. This rule applies to weekends as well as weekdays. "Therefore, since we are surrounded by so great a cloud of witnesses, let us rid ourselves of every burden and sin that clings to us and persevere in running the race that lies before us while keeping our eyes fixed on Jesus, the leader and perfecter of faith." (Hebrews 12:1-2a)

Communion with the Saints,
A Family Preparation Program for First
Communion and Beyond in the Spirit of St. Therese

Study Guide

Monday, Week 1 (Day 1)

Parents: Read pages vii-xiv today in *The Story of a Family, The Home of St. Thérèse of Lisieux* by Fr. Stéphane-Joseph Piat, O.F.M.

High School and Middle School Students: Read the Introduction (Foreword) and Prologue in *The Story of a Soul, The Autobiography of St. Therese of Lisieux.*

First Communicants: Begin your First Communion journal by completing "Day 1" in your journal today.

Family Read Aloud: Read Chapter 1 of *The Little Flower, The Story of St. Therese of the Child Jesus* by Mary Fabyan Windeatt.

Chapter 1—In Which Therese Is Born and Thrives

Comprehension Questions/Narration Prompts

1. Why did some people think that the marriage of Therese's parents was a mistake?
2. Why did Therese's parents name all of their children—even the boys—"Marie"? Why was it important for them to have a boy?
3. What day was Therese born? What was her full name?
4. Why was Therese sent to live in the country with a nurse?

Discussion Topics

After the death of his two sons, Therese's father stated, "The boys will pray for us. Just think! They went to God without one sin on their souls!" (page 3) Discuss the Church's teaching of the communion of saints as it applies to this quotation. Include the three groups of saints included in this doctrine as well as how each group helps each other.

Growing in Holiness

"Everyone marveled at the wonderful way in which Papa and Mama accepted these fresh trials. Death had called four times in twelve years, yet the Martin house was still a cheerful place." (page 4) Is your house a cheerful place? What immediate steps can you take to help it be a more cheerful place? Consider at least two positive actions that you can take toward this goal as well as at least two things that you can stop doing in order to help your house be full of Christian joy.

Optional Catechism Lessons

1. First Communicants should complete one of the following:
   a. In *The New Saint Joseph First Communion Catechism*, read Lesson 1 **or**
   b. In *Jesus Our Life* from the Faith and Life series, read Lesson 1; review questions 1-4; review the "Words to Know" using the definitions that start on page 141.

2. Older siblings should review Lesson 24 in *The New Saint Joseph Baltimore Catechism* on baptism. In the *Catechism of the Catholic Church (CCC)*, this would be text paragraphs 1213-1274 (252-264) or the summary at paragraphs 1275-1284. Be sure to review the role of godparents as outlined in text paragraph 1255 (259).

Tuesday, Week 1 (Day 2)

Parents: Read pages 3-10 in *The Story of a Family*.
High School and Middle School Students: Read the first chapter in *Story of a Soul*.
First Communicants: Complete "Day 2" in your First Communion journal.
Family Read Aloud: Read Chapter 2 of *The Little Flower*.

Chapter 2—In Which Therese Begins To Love Jesus

Comprehension Questions/Narration Prompts
1. By what pet name did Therese's father call her?
2. What did Mr. and Mrs. Martin do for a living?
3. At what age did Therese decide to become a nun?

Discussion Topics
1. What are some of Therese's faults? Give examples of each from the story.
2. What plan does three-year-old Therese enact to become a saint?
3. Explain the meaning of this statement: "I will make you happy not in this world but in the next." (page 20)

Growing in Holiness
If you have a set of St. Therese sacrifice beads, use them to keep track of the sacrifices you make and the good deeds you do each day. See how many times each day you can please the Little Jesus by saying humbling yourself and saying "Yes" to God. In the space provided in the journal (lower right-hand side of each day's entry), enter the number of sacrifices you make each day.

Optional Catechism Lessons
1. First Communicants should complete one of the following:
    a. Answer questions at the end of Lesson 1 in *The New Saint Joseph First Communion Catechism*; begin memorization of catechism questions 1-4 **or**
    b. Read Lesson 2 in *Jesus Our Life* from the Faith and Life series. Review questions 5-7 and the "Words to Know."
2. By this statement, ". . . but I want you (her mother and father) to go to Heaven" (page 12), Therese shows that even at the age of three, she had a good understanding of the purpose of man's existence. Older siblings should review Lesson 1 in *The New Saint Joseph Baltimore Catechism* as well as text paragraphs 27-28, 293-294, 355-58, 1718, 185-87, 198, 239, 268, 279, 314, 325-27, 358, 422-24, 430, 484-88, 596, 619-623, 629-30, 636-37, 656-58, 665-67, and 680-82 (36, 51, 53, 59, 66, 79, and 135) in the *CCC*.

Wednesday, Week 1 (Day 3)

Parents: Read pages 11-21 in *The Story of a Family*.
High School and Middle School Students: Read the second chapter in *Story of a Soul*.
First Communicants: Complete "Day 3" in your First Communion journal.
Family Read Aloud: Read Chapter 3 of *The Little Flower*.

Chapter 3—In Which Therese Loses Her Mother and Continues to Grow in the Good God's Grace

Comprehension Questions/Narration Prompts

1. After the death of her mother, Therese and her family move to Lisieux. State the name of their new home there as well as the meaning of this name.
2. Why were Carmelites "hidden from the world"? (page 25)
3. What effect did the priest's blessing have on Therese's rosary beads?

Discussion Topics

1. Describe the activities in the Martin house on Sunday, Therese's favorite day of the week. Compare and contrast these activities with the activities in your house on this day.

2. What do the terms "merit of sacrifice" and "merit of obedience" as used by Pauline on page 31 mean?

Growing in Holiness

Therese and her father made a habit of visiting Jesus in the tabernacle of the churches they would pass on their daily walks. Choose a time of day or a day of the week to visit Jesus as they did. Memorize the prayer Therese recited after her first confession (page 28) and recite it before the tabernacle—or in times of temptation: "My God, I give You my heart. May it please You to accept it, so that no creature can take possession of it but You alone, my good Jesus!" Note in your journal each day in the space provided on the lower left-hand page the number of prayers recited each day.

Optional Catechism Lessons

1. First Communicants should complete one of the following:
    a. Write catechism questions 1-4 from *The New Saint Joseph First Communion Catechism* on index cards and review **or**
    b. Read Lesson 3 in *Jesus Our Life* from the Faith and Life series; review questions 1-9 and all the "Words to Know" studied to date.
2. Therese received the Sacrament of Penance when she was six years old; she states, "I had been well instructed as to the meaning of Confession." (page 27) Older siblings can review Lesson 29 in *The New Saint Joseph Baltimore Catechism* to reinforce their understanding of this sacrament. Corresponding text paragraphs in the *Catechism of the Catholic Church* include 1440-1470 (296-312).

Thursday, Week 1 (Day 4)
Parents: Read pages 22-32 in *The Story of a Family*.
High School and Middle School Students: Read the third chapter in *Story of a Soul*.
First Communicants: Complete "Day 4" in your First Communion journal.
Family Read Aloud: Read Chapter 4 of *The Little Flower*.

Chapter 4—In Which Therese Attends School and Becomes Very Ill

Comprehension Questions/Narration Prompts
1. How old was Therese when she began to attend school? Where did she attend?
2. What was the name Pauline received upon her admission to Carmel? What was the name Therese was to receive should she later be admitted?
3. Describe the spiritual battle that took place immediately before Therese's cure from her mysterious illness.

Discussion Topics
1. Discuss several possible meanings of the "vision" Therese had of her father.
2. Father Domin, the chaplain at the Benedictine convent, called Therese his "Little Doctor." (page 34) Why was this a prophetic statement?

Growing in Holiness
"Priests would be her (Pauline's) particular care. She would offer her life that God might bless the world with many good and holy priests." (page 36) As there are now fewer cloistered nuns to pray for priests, be sure to pray daily for "good and holy priests." After each decade of the rosary, add the following prayer: "God our Father, please send us holy priests."

Optional Catechism Lessons
1. First Communicants should complete one of the following:
   a. Ask someone to read with you the story of creation from the Bible, Genesis chapter 1; continue memorization of catechism questions 1-4 from the flash cards. Begin memorization of the prayers found at the beginning and end of this book **or**
   b. Read Lesson 4 in *Jesus Our Life* from the Faith and Life series. Review questions 10-11 and the "Words to Know."
2. Older siblings should review Lessons 21 and 22 in *The New Saint Joseph Baltimore Catechism* on the commandments of the Church.

Friday, Week 1 (Day 5)
Parents: Read pages 32-41 in *The Story of a Family*.
High School and Middle School Students: Read the fourth chapter in *Story of a Soul*.
First Communicants: Complete "Day 5" in your First Communion journal.
Family Read Aloud: Read Chapter 5 of *The Little Flower*.

Chapter 5—In Which Therese Receives Her First Communion and Confirmation, and Her Prayers for Peace Are Answered

Comprehension Questions/Narration Prompts
1. How old was Therese when she received her first Holy Communion? How did she prepare? List the resolutions Therese made after her First Holy Communion.
2. How old was Therese when she received the Sacrament of Confirmation? For which gift did she feel a special need?
3. What was the second miracle Therese felt was performed in her life?

Discussion Topics
1. Discuss how Therese felt at the reception of Our Lord in Holy Communion.
2. Explain Therese's idea of our journey toward or away from heaven.
3. Expand on Therese's idea of our union with God as compared to a drop of rain in the ocean.

Growing in Holiness
". . . I had stumbled on the real meaning of meditation." (page 42) Set aside ten minutes each day to mediate upon the mysteries of God and our faith. If necessary when beginning, use the verses of the Gospels to provide a starting point and to keep focused. Remember too the words of St. Philip Neri, "The best preparation for prayer is to read the lives of the saints . . . And to pause whenever you feel your heart touched with devotion."

Optional Catechism Lessons
1. First Communicants should complete one of the following:
   a. Complete memorization of catechism questions 1-4 from Lesson 1 in the First Communion Catechism; continue memory work on the prayers **or**
   b. Review Lessons 1-4 in *Jesus Our Life* by reviewing questions 1-11 as well as the "Words to Know" from each lesson; begin memory work on the prayers contained at the back of the book.
2. Older siblings should review Lesson 25 on the Sacrament of Confirmation in *The New Saint Joseph Baltimore Catechism*. Review the following text paragraphs from the *Catechism of the Catholic Church*: 1121, 1285, 1289, 1297-1314—or the "In Brief" section 1315-21—and 2472 (265-270).

Saturday, Week 1 and Sunday, Week 2 (Days 6 and 7)
Parents: Finish any reading necessary so that you are prepared to begin on page 42 in *The Story of a Family* on Monday.

High School and Middle School Students: Read the meditational readings in the Reading Schedule for High School and Middle School Students on pages 77-78 below.

First Communicants: Complete an entry in your journal each day this weekend.

Family: Choose an activity in the "Weekend Projects" section beginning on page 103.

Monday, Week 2 (Day 8)

Parents: Read pages 42-49 in *The Story of a Family*.

High School and Middle School Students: Read the fifth chapter in *Story of a Soul*.

First Communicants: Complete "Day 8" in your First Communion journal.

Family Read Aloud: Read Chapter 6 of *The Little Flower*.

Chapter 6—In Which Therese's Soul Thirsts for Sinners and Grows in Grace

Comprehension Questions/Narration Prompts

1. What prompted Therese's longing to suffer for the conversion of sinners?
2. Why did Therese join the Carmelites as opposed to a missionary order?
3. Therese delayed speaking to her father for several weeks about her decision to enter Carmel. Why?
4. Who were opposed to Therese' entrance into Carmel at the age of fourteen?

Discussion Topics

1. "Conversion" is a word most often used by Christians to refer to a change from a pagan or secular lifestyle to a Christian one. In this chapter, Therese speaks of her conversion as a change in attitude within her already-Christian lifestyle. Relate the conversion story of Therese on Christmas of 1886. How did it happen and what was the result? What behavior and attitudes changed?
2. Explain the difference this conversion made in Therese's life. Outwardly, she had not changed; but inwardly, her attitude was very different. How was she now leading a life much like the nuns in Carmel?
3. Tell the story of Therese's "first child of grace", Pranzini.

Growing in Holiness

Until her entrance into Carmel, Therese wanted to "Pray for sinners. Look about and do good." (page 58) She felt that her first duty in her new life of charity was toward her own family. (page 54) Note some of the activities Therese engaged in, and try to imitate her within your own house. Think of ways you can bring love and kindness to your siblings and parents. Look for opportunities to imitate Therese in acts of charity with your family.

Optional Catechism Lessons

1. First Communicants should complete one of the following:
   a. Read Lesson 2, "God Is Great" and Lesson 3 "The Blessed Trinity" in *The New Saint Joseph First Communion Catechism* **or**
   b. Read Lesson 5 in *Jesus Our Life* from the Faith and Life series; review questions 12-15 and the "Words to Know." Begin the recite the Guardian Angel prayer each night at bedtime.
2. In this chapter, Therese prepares herself for Carmel by growing in grace. Review Lesson 23 in *The New Saint Joseph Baltimore Catechism* on the sacraments—our channels of grace. Corresponding text paragraphs in the *CCC* include 1113-16, 1121-23, 1129, 1131-34, and 1211-12 (146, 224-232, 237-38, 250-51, 295, and 321).

Tuesday, Week 2 (Day 9)

Parents: Read pages 50-58 in *The Story of a Family*.

High School and Middle School Students: Read the sixth chapter in *Story of a Soul*.

First Communicants: Complete "Day 9" in your First Communion journal.

Family Read Aloud: Read Chapter 7 of *The Little Flower*.

Chapter 7—In Which Therese Speaks to the Pope Regarding Entrance to Carmel

Comprehension Questions/Narration Prompts

1. What question was settled in Paris at the church of Our Lady of Victories?
2. State the prayer Therese offered while in the Coliseum.
3. What was Pope Leo XIII's reaction to Therese's request to enter Carmel at fifteen?

Discussion Topics

1. Therese and her family spent six days visiting the principal attractions of Rome before Therese's audience with the Holy Father. List the sites seen by Therese and her family and state the significance of each.
2. Narrate Therese's encounter with Pope Leo XIII from his point of view. Use "I" to describe this scene as the Holy Father would remember it.

Growing in Holiness

If your family is not yet consecrated to the Sacred Heart of Jesus—or if you have not yet made a personal consecration—consider doing so now. Our Lord has said that He will bless those homes where an image of His Heart is exposed and venerated. He has promised to give peace to their families and abundantly bless all their undertakings. He has further promised refuge in life and especially at the hour of death. For this consecration, a priest should bless a statue, picture, or icon of the Sacred Heart. After it is set in a place of honor, a consecration prayer such as the following should be recited.

> Most Sweet Jesus, humbly at your feet, we (make) the consecration of our family to Your Divine Heart. Be our King forever! In You we have full and entire confidence. May Your spirit penetrate our thoughts, our desires, our words, and our works. Bless our undertakings, share in our joys, in our trials, and in our labors. Grant us to know You better, to love You more, to serve You without faltering.
>
> By the Immaculate Heart of Mary, Queen of Peace, set up Your Kingdom in our country. Enter closely the midst of our families and make them Your own through the solemn enthronement of Your Sacred Heart, so that soon one cry may resound from home to home: May the triumphant Heart of Jesus be everywhere loved, blessed, and glorified forever! Honor and glory be to the Sacred Heart of Jesus and Mary in union with St. Joseph! Sacred Heart, protect our families. (Jerome F. Coniker—Compiler, *Family Consecration Prayer & Meditation Book, Divine Mercy Edition*, p. 84)

Renew this consecration annually or monthly at Mass on each first Friday. You may make a daily consecration by using the following prayer each morning:

Sacred Heart of Jesus, remember that we are consecrated and belong to You. Bless and protect us all. May our home be a shrine of Your love and Your grace. Strengthen the bond of affection that unites us together. Help us to bear one another's burdens in peace and harmony and unselfishness. Keep us always near to You and to Your blessed mother. Amen.

Optional Catechism Lessons
1. First Communicants should complete one of the following:
   a. Answer the questions at the end of Lessons 2 and 3 in *The New Saint Joseph First Communion Catechism*; begin memorization of catechism questions 5-13 **or**
   b. Read Lesson 6 in *Jesus Our Life* from the Faith and Life series; review questions 16 and 17 and the "Words to Know."
2. Review Lesson 27 in *The New Saint Joseph Baltimore Catechism* on the Mass. Corresponding text paragraphs in the *Catechism of the Catholic Church* include 1330, 1357 and 1544-1545. If desired, the entire section on the Eucharist, 1322-1405 (271-294), or only the "In Brief" section in text paragraphs 1406-1419 can be reviewed.

Wednesday, Week 2 (Day 10)
Parents: Read pages 58-65 in *The Story of a Family*.
High School and Middle School Students: Read the first half of Chapter 7 in *Story of a Soul*.
First Communicants: Complete "Day 10" in your First Communion journal.
Family Read Aloud: Read Chapter 8 of *The Little Flower*.

Chapter 8—In Which Therese Begins Her Life as a Carmelite Nun

Comprehension Questions/Narration Prompts
1. How long did Therese's trip to Rome take?
2. Why did Mother Gonzago wait until after Easter before admitting Therese to Carmel?
3. Why did Therese wish to enter Carmel?
4. What duty was Therese given for exercise at Carmel?

Discussion Topics
1. Discuss how Therese gave up her will to the Will of God. Watch for further references of this practice.
2. Further detail the lesson Therese learned from the lamb given to her by her father. How can you apply this lesson in your life? How is this lesson related to the required use of the word "our" instead of "my" in the cloister?

Growing in Holiness
"I kept silent. A good religious is not expected to make excuses for herself, even when she is in the right." (page 82. Apply this to your life by not defending yourself against charges, righteous or not. Neither should you make excuses for your behavior or actions. This is especially difficult in a family setting, but remember the graces that will flow from this sacrifice. Offer these sacrifices for the conversion of a great many sinners.

Optional Catechism Lessons
1. First Communicants should complete one of the following:
    a. Write catechism questions 5-13 from *The New Saint Joseph First Communion Catechism* on index cards and review along with questions 1-4 **or**
    b. Read Lesson 7 in *Jesus Our Life* from the Faith and Life series; review the "Words to Know."
2. Father Pichon declared that Therese had never committed a single mortal sin. Review Lesson 6 in *The New Saint Joseph Baltimore Catechism* regarding actual sin. Read the following text paragraphs in the *Catechism of the Catholic Church*: 1854-1866 (391-396).

Thursday, Week 2 (Day 11)
Parents: Read pages 66-75 in *The Story of a Family*.
High School and Middle School Students: Read the second half of the seventh chapter in *Story of a Soul*.
First Communicants: Complete "Day 11" in your First Communion journal.
Family Read Aloud: Read Chapter 9 of *The Little Flower*.

Chapter 9—In Which Therese Continues to Lead a Life of Sacrifice for the Salvation of Sinners

Comprehension Questions/Narration Prompts
1. When did Therese receive the habit of the Carmelite order? How old was she?
2. What was Therese's special charge in the chapel?
3. Who delayed Therese's Profession of Solemn Vows?

Discussion Topics
1. Expand on Therese's statement that perpetual sacrifice is the "coin with which sinners could be ransomed." (page 93) What sacrifices can you make to ransom sinners today? Do not "let this wonderful coin slip through (your) fingers."
2. Discern the meaning of this statement of Therese's: "Most people find it easy to love the little Christ Child . . . but the true Christian never separates Bethlehem from Calvary." (page 96) How can you use this insight to enrich your spiritual life?

Growing in Holiness
Re-read Therese's description of her Little Way from page 88: "I gave myself and all my actions to our Lord . . ." Review too from page 95: ". . . no anxieties or trials of daily life are too small to be offered to God. For instance, I was often tired and cold. Well, I would offer my discomfort to God the Father, in union with Christ's sufferings and death on Calvary." Remember her attitude regarding her missing lamp and her beautiful jug. Live the way of St. Therese—not by doing great things but by doing your daily duty with great love. Consider too St. Faustina's quotation, "I will not allow myself to be so absorbed in the whirlwind of work as to forget God." (Diary, 82)

Optional Catechism Lessons

1. First Communicants should complete one of the following:
   a. Review "Some Things I See in Church"; if possible, go to your parish church and find these things—what else can you find? Continue memorization of catechism questions 1-13 from the flash cards **or**
   b. Ask someone to read you the stories of Noah, Abraham, Isaac, and David from a children's story Bible. Draw a picture of one of these stories.
2. Older siblings should review Lesson 31 on confession in *The New Saint Joseph Baltimore Catechism*. Corresponding text paragraphs in the *CCC* include 1440-60 (303-306) and 1468-1470 (432).

Friday, Week 2 (Day 12)

Parents: Read pages 76-84 in *The Story of a Family*.

High School and Middle School Students: Read the eighth chapter in *Story of a Soul*.

First Communicants: Complete "Day 12" in your First Communion journal.

Family Read Aloud: Read Chapter 10 of *The Little Flower*.

Chapter 10—In Which Therese Professes Her Vows and Lives Her Vocation

Comprehension Questions/Narration Prompts

1. What doubt did Therese have the night before her Profession Day? What caused this doubt?
2. What two thoughts concerning her vocation consoled Therese after the death of her father?
3. What privilege came to Therese because of the influenza epidemic in 1891?

Discussion Topics

Therese notes four new duties she was assigned. What were these duties? How can each of these duties give glory to God?

Growing in Holiness

"He accepted my sufferings, offered in union with those of His Son on Calvary, and applied their merit to souls too lazy or indifferent to pray for themselves." (page 102) Our Lady of Fatima appeared on August 19, 1917—about twenty years after Therese made this statement—and implored us to "Pray! Pray a great deal and make sacrifices for sinners, for many souls go to Hell for not having someone to pray and make sacrifices for them." With the shortage of cloistered nuns and monks to pray and make sacrifices, this statement is far more ominous today. Many souls are lost, as there is no one to pray and make sacrifices for them. Pray and make sacrifices each day for those souls who do not pray for themselves that they might be given the grace to convert and obtain heaven.

Optional Catechism Lessons

1. First Communicants should complete one of the following:
    a. Complete memorization of catechism questions 1-13 from the flash cards; continue memorization of the prayers. Draw a picture of the Blessed Trinity using the picture on page 16 as a guide or creating a design of your own **or**
    b. Review questions 1-17 as well as the "Words to Know" from Lessons 1-7 in *Jesus Our Life*; continue to work on the memorization of the prayers from the end of the book.
2. Older siblings should review Lesson 28 in *The New Saint Joseph Baltimore Catechism*, which covers the regulations on receiving Holy Communion.

Saturday, Week 2 and Week 3, Sunday (Days 13 and 14)

Parents: Finish any reading necessary so that you are prepared to begin on page 84 in *The Story of a Family* on Monday.

High School and Middle School Students: Read the meditational readings on page 78.

First Communicants: Complete an entry in your journal each day this weekend.

Family: Choose an activity in the "Weekend Projects" section of this guide.

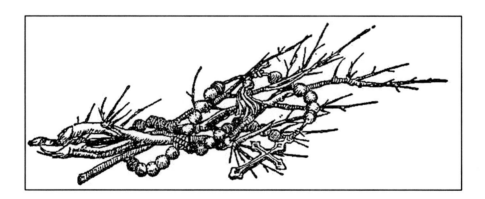

Monday, Week 3 (Day 15)
Parents: Read pages 84-92 in *The Story of a Family*.
High School and Middle School Students: Read the ninth chapter in *Story of a Soul*.
First Communicants: Complete "Day 15" in your First Communion journal.
Family Read Aloud: Read Chapter 11 of *The Little Flower*.

Chapter 11—In Which Therese Begins to Write Her Autobiography

Comprehension Questions/Narration Prompts
1. In what method did Therese instruct the novices under her care?
2. One request that Therese made to our Lord on her Profession Day was for Leonie to be given a religious vocation and join the Visitation order. When was this petition was granted?
3. Why was it difficult for Celine to enter Carmel?
4. Who ordered Therese to write down her childhood memories and why?
5. Who gave Therese the title of "*The Little Flower*"?

Discussion Topics
1. Describe the "Little Way" of Therese. Compare and contrast it with the "Great Way."
2. Explain why Therese gave her book of memories the title she did. What is the symbolism and history behind the title of "*The Little Flower*"?

Growing in Holiness
Therese asked the Queen of Heaven to bless her new work—the writing of her childhood memories. Remember to ask this same spiritual assistance when you begin writing. Perhaps you would like to begin a journal of your own childhood memories and favors granted from God. Place the initials "J.M.J." at the top of each page you write to ask the blessing of Jesus, Mary, and Joseph in your work. This can make even your schoolwork an offering to the glory of God.

Optional Catechism Lessons
1. First Communicants should complete one of the following:
   a. Read Lesson 4 "The First Sins" in the First Communion Catechism **or**
   b. Read Lesson 8 in *Jesus Our Life* from the Faith and Life series; review the "Words to Know" and the Ten Commandments.
2. Therese had prayed that her father's earthly sufferings would serve as his purgatory. Review Lesson 14 in *The New Saint Joseph Baltimore Catechism* on the Resurrection and the life everlasting. Older siblings may read text paragraphs 1011, 1030-1032 and 1472 (131 and 202-216) in the *Catechism of the Catholic Church*.

Tuesday, Week 3 (Day 16)

Parents: Read pages 93-106 today in *The Story of a Family*.

High School and Middle School Students: Read the first half of the tenth chapter in *Story of a Soul*.

First Communicants: Complete "Day 16" in your First Communion journal.

Family Read Aloud: Read Chapter 12 of *The Little Flower*.

Chapter 12—In Which Therese Continues to Guide Souls along the Path of Spiritual Childhood

Comprehension Questions/Narration Prompts

1. What offering did Therese, weak and little, make to the Heavenly Father?
2. What is the only fear Therese had?
3. List three important events in Therese's life that took place in 1895.
4. State why Therese was so loved to correspond with the priestly missionaries.

Discussion Topics

1. Discuss Therese's view of God that is in direct opposition to most people's view. (See pages 122 and 123.)
2. "The little white flower would flourish in its springtime only." (page 123) What do you think this means?

Growing in Holiness

"When I think of all I have to acquire!" cried a novice one day. . . . "You mean all that you have to lose," [Therese] said. "You are trying to climb a mountain, whereas God wishes you to descend." (page 128) Sometimes we concentrate on obtaining holiness and acquiring virtue, when perhaps we should think of losing ourselves—our self-will, our worldliness. We need to fall as grains of wheat (John 12:24) and die to ourselves. We too can offer an oblation as Therese did. Compose an oblation of your own and pray it carefully each morning and in times of temptation. Perhaps you could tell God that each day you will offer less to Him, that each day by His Holy Love you wish to be made smaller until finally there is nothing left of you except holy emptiness that God can fill if He wishes, or not, according to His Will.

Optional Catechism Lessons

1. First Communicants should complete one of the following:
    a. Answer questions at the end of Lesson 4 in *The New Saint Joseph First Communion Catechism*; begin memorization of catechism questions 22-27 **or**
    b. Read Lesson 9 in *Jesus Our Life* from the Faith and Life series; review questions 18-19 as well as the "Words to Know." Begin memorization of the Ten Commandments as found on page 36.
2. Therese speaks of the "Feast of the Most Holy Trinity." (page 122) Older siblings should review Lesson 3 in *The New Saint Joseph Baltimore Catechism* on the Trinity. Corresponding text paragraphs in the *Catechism of the Catholic Church* include 234-237, 249-256, and 261-267 (44-49). When is this feast now celebrated?

Wednesday, Week 3 (Day 17)

Parents: Read pages 107-116 in *The Story of a Family.*

High School and Middle School Students: Read the second half of the tenth chapter in *Story of a Soul.*

First Communicants: Complete "Day 17" in your First Communion journal.

Family Read Aloud: Read Chapter 13 of *The Little Flower.*

Chapter 13—In Which Therese Contracts Tuberculosis and Dreams of Going to Heaven Soon

Comprehension Questions/Narration Prompts
1. How long does Therese feel she has yet to live?
2. What does Marie ask Therese to do in order to help Marie's willingness to suffer?
3. What does Therese claim is one of her greatest sufferings at Carmel?

Discussion Topics
1. Retell the dream Therese had on the night of May 10, 1896.
2. Describe Therese's temptation of faith.

Growing in Holiness
Therese states that she made a novena to ask God for the favor of going to the Orient as a missionary. Pray a novena asking God for some favor you wish Him to grant to you. (Remember a novena is a prayer extended over a period of nine days and said for some special petition or occasion.)

Optional Catechism Lessons
1. First Communicants should complete one of the following:
   a. Write catechism questions 22-27 from *The New Saint Joseph First Communion Catechism* on index cards and review **or**
   b. Read Lesson 10 in *Jesus Our Life* from the Faith and Life series; review questions 20-21 as well as the "Words to Know."
2. Therese often called God the "Father of love and mercy." (page 139) Older siblings should review Lesson 38 in *The New Saint Joseph Baltimore Catechism (Book No. 2* only) on the Our Father. In the *Catechism of the Catholic Church,* this lesson is covered in text paragraphs 2759-2865 (544, 569, and 578-598) and summarized in text paragraphs 2759, 2761-2766, 2797-2802, and 2857-2865.

Thursday, Week 3 (Day 18)

Parents: Read pages 117-127 in *The Story of a Family.*

High School and Middle School Students: Read the first half of the eleventh chapter in *Story of a Soul.*

First Communicants: Complete "Day 18" in your First Communion journal.

Family Read Aloud: Read Chapter 14 of *The Little Flower.*

Chapter 14—In Which Therese and Her Sisters Prepare for the Death of Therese

Comprehension Questions/Narration Prompts
1. What did Therese believe people need do to be truly free and happy?
2. For what did Marie hope when she placed the statue of the Blessed Virgin in her sister Therese's room in the Infirmary?
3. By what way does Therese wish to lead souls?
4. What three predictions did Therese make before her death?

Discussion Topics
1. "Well, this little Sister is very amiable, but surely she has done nothing much since coming here." (page 144) These words spoken by one of the sisters at Carmel tell us that it is difficult to judge sanctity by outward appearances. What do you feel are some of the characteristics of saintliness?
2. Therese originally wrote her childhood memories ending with events of 1895; this took her one full year to complete. Next, she wrote a manuscript for Marie on her vocation of love, which Therese wrote in three days. Now Pauline has requested that she write another addition to her autobiography. In June before her death, Therese wrote two rather lengthy chapters covering her life as a religious. In addition, Pauline recorded many of the sayings of Therese in the months before Therese's death. This material makes up another entire book entitled *Therese of Lisieux, Her Last Conversations*. In the first person, write briefly how you (as Therese) feel knowing that many people will read about your life and your relationship with God. How would it feel to know that countless souls might not only be brought into a closer relationship with God, but might also be saved for all eternity by your witness and example?

Growing in Holiness
Re-read the first two paragraphs on page 148. Consider at least two rights or privileges that you have. Do not make the mistake of taking these "rights" for granted. Be aware that we all owe our "very existence to God's love." It is a mistake to get indignant or possessive of "rights" that are not really ours.

Optional Catechism Lessons
1. First Communicants should complete one of the following:
    a. Act out the story of Adam and Eve. Continue memorization of catechism questions 1-13 and 22-27 from the flash cards **or**
    b. Ask someone to read to you the stories of the Annunciation and the birth of Jesus in the Bible (Luke 1:26-38 and 2:1-20). Read the Ten Commandments and the Two Great Commandments in the Bible (Exodus 20:1-17 and Matthew 22:34-40). Continue memorization of the Ten Commandments.
2. Older siblings should review Lesson 10 in *The New Saint Joseph Baltimore Catechism* on the virtues and the Holy Spirit especially the theological virtues of faith, hope, and charity. Read corresponding text paragraphs in the *CCC*: 1999-2005, 1812-32—or the "In Brief" section 1840-45—736, 1716-24, and 1803-24 (377-390).

Friday, Week 3 (Day 19)

Parents: Read pages 128-138 in *The Story of a Family*.

High School and Middle School Students: Read the second half of the eleventh chapter, and the Epilogue, in *Story of a Soul*.

First Communicants: Complete "Day 19" in your First Communion journal.

Family Read Aloud: Read Chapter 15 of *The Little Flower*.

Chapter 15—In Which Therese Continues Doing Good upon Earth

Comprehension Questions/Narration Prompts

1. In what way did Therese wish to imitate Christ to the last?
2. What did Therese expect others to discover when they read her book?
3. What did Celine and Therese see as a sign of Therese's impending death? Why?

Discussion Topics

1. Explain how "heaven" and "childhood" go together.
2. On page 157, Therese gives a definition of holiness. Read and re-read this. Use a dictionary if necessary to check out the meaning of any words you do not understand. Rephrase this definition of holiness into your own words.

Growing in Holiness

"Few people realize how furiously the Devil fights to drag souls to Hell, all during our life but most especially at the hour of our death." (page 159) Make an effort to mediate more deeply on the words of the Hail Mary the next time you pray them. Pray often that God will grant you the grace to obtain a happy death. Perhaps too you could begin praying each day at three o'clock in the afternoon—the hour of God's Mercy—for those souls who will die today that they too may attain heaven to love God for all eternity.

Optional Catechism Lessons

1. First Communicants should complete one of the following:
   a. Complete memorization of catechism questions 22-27 from Lesson 4 in *The New Saint Joseph First Communion Catechism*; review questions 1-13; continue memorization of the prayers **or**
   b. Review Lessons 8-10 in *Jesus Our Life* by reviewing questions 18-21 as well as the "Words to Know" from each lesson; continue memorization of the guardian angel prayer and the Ten Commandments as necessary
2. Therese wanted to imitate Christ to the very last. She united her death to His on the cross. Older siblings should review Lesson 8 in *The New Saint Joseph Baltimore Catechism* on the redemption. Corresponding text paragraphs in the *Catechism of the Catholic Church* include 571-73, 601, 618, 619-23, 629-30, and 636-37 (65, 112, and 219).

Saturday, Week 3 and Week 4, Sunday (Days 20 and 21)

Parents: Finish any reading necessary so that you are prepared to begin on page 139 in *The Story of a Family* on Monday.

High School and Middle School Students: Read the meditational readings on pages 78-79.

First Communicants: Complete an entry in your journal each day this weekend.

Family: Choose an activity in the "Weekend Projects" section of this guide.

Monday, Week 4 (Day 22)
Parents: Read pages 139-149 in *The Story of a Family*.
High School and Middle School Students: Read the meditational reading on page 79.
First Communicants: Complete "Day 22" in your First Communion journal.
Family Read Aloud: Read Chapter 1 of *The Children of Fatima and the Message of Our Lady to the World* by Mary Fabyan Windeatt.

Chapter 1—In Which the Angel of Peace Teaches the Shepherd Children to Pray

Comprehension Questions/Narration Prompts
1. State the names and ages of each of the children who were present for the appearances of the angel at Fatima.
2. Name some of the things the children did for amusement as they watched their parents' sheep each day.
3. What was Francisco's attitude toward the rosary and church?
4. How many times did the angel appear to the children? State the times and give a brief summary of each visit.

Discussion Topics
1. Review each of the two prayers that the angel taught the children; the first is commonly called the "Pardon Prayer", and the second is the "Angel's Prayer." Discuss each phrase of each of these prayers, putting each of them into your own words while keeping the meaning and intent of each prayer intact.
2. Jacinta and Francisco were surprised to have the angel offer Communion to them as "they knew only a very little of the catechism!" (page 7) Consider the following statement taken from the Decree on First Communion as issued by Pope Pius X on August 8, 1910: "A full and perfect knowledge of Christian doctrine is not necessary either for First Confession or for First Communion. Afterwards, however, the child will be obliged to learn gradually the entire Catechism according to his ability. The knowledge of religion which is required in a child in order to be properly prepared to receive First Communion is such that he will understand according to his capacity those Mysteries of faith which are necessary as a means of salvation and that he can distinguish between the Bread of the Eucharist and ordinary, material bread, and thus he may receive Holy Communion with a devotion becoming his years." What knowledge was required of Jacinta and Francisco that they may properly receive Communion? Discuss whether all three children received Communion equally—did all three truly receive the Body, Blood, Soul, and Divinity of Jesus? Discuss the following stanzas of St. Thomas Aquinas' great hymn composed for the Feast of Corpus Christi, *Lauda Sion*:

> Here in outward signs are hidden,
> Priceless things, to sense forbidden;
> Signs, not things, are all we see—
> Flesh from bread, and Blood from wine;
> Yet is Christ, in either sign,
> All entire confessed to be.
> They too who of Him partake
> Sever not, nor rend, nor break,
> But entire their Lord receive,
> Whether one or thousands eat,
> All receive the selfsame meat,
> Nor the less for others leave.

(See answer key for more information on receiving Holy Communion from an angel.)

Growing in Holiness

Memorize both prayers that the angel taught to the shepherd children. Recite these prayers daily three times each with your head bowed to the ground or floor as the angel did. The first prayer is an excellent prayer to recite before the Blessed Sacrament or a crucifix, and the prayer to the Holy Trinity makes a good offertory prayer when recited immediately before the reception of Holy Communion. These prayers have been given to us so we can make reparation for our sins and the sins of all humanity; pray them often to help fulfill the requests of our Lady of Fatima.

Optional Catechism Lessons

1. First Communicants should complete one of the following:
    a. In the First Communion Catechism, read Lesson 5 "Our Own Sins" **or**
    b. In *Jesus Our Life* from the Faith and Life series, read Lesson 11; review questions 22-25 as well as the "Words to Know."
2. Older siblings should review the Church's teaching on angels in Lesson 4 in *The New Saint Joseph Baltimore Catechism*. Corresponding text paragraphs in the *Catechism of the Catholic Church* include 311, 328-36, 350-51, 391-95 and 1034 (59-61, 74, and 209).

Tuesday, Week 4 (Day 23)

Parents: Read 149-159 pages in *The Story of a Family*.
High School and Middle School Students: Read the meditational reading on page 79.
First Communicants: Complete "Day 23" in your First Communion journal.
Family Read Aloud: Read Chapter 2 of *The Children of Fatima*.

Chapter 2—In Which Our Lady Visits the Shepherd Children

Comprehension Questions/Narration Prompts

1. When was the first appearance of our Lady to the shepherd children?
2. Who heard and spoke to our Lady?
3. Why did the children want to keep the visit of the lady a secret?

Discussion Topics

1. When Francisco asked Lucia how making small sacrifices can convert sinners, she replied, "Don't ask questions. The angel told us what to do, and we should obey him." (page 11) Obedience is important, as it is how we follow the Fourth Commandment. But perhaps you can construct a response to Francisco that more fully answers his question. Review the doctrine of the communion of saints. Read Hebrews 10:24, Philippians 1:29, Philippians 2:14, and Colossians 1:24 before preparing your response.

2. Prepare an outline or chart in which all the messages of our Lady as well as the messages of the angel can be included. Outline the dates and messages of the three appearances of the angel; add this first message of our Lady including the date and the three things she asked of the children. Add to this outline/chart each time our Lady appears to the children. Discuss how you can apply our Lady's message today.

Growing in Holiness

Our Lady states that the young girl Amelia will be in Purgatory until the end of the world. (page 13) Recite the following "Prayer for Daily Neglects" which is from a Poor Clare nun. Shortly after her death, this nun appeared to her Abbess and told her, "I went straight to Heaven, for, by means of this prayer recited every evening, I paid all my debts."

 Eternal Father, I offer Thee the Sacred Heart of Jesus, with all its love, all its sufferings, and all its merits.

 First—To expiate all the sins I have committed this day and during all my life, (say one Glory Be)

 Second—To purify the good I have done poorly this day and during all my life, (say one Glory Be)

 Third—To supply for the good I ought to have done, and that I have neglected this day and all my life, (say one Glory Be) Amen.

Optional Catechism Lessons

1. First Communicants should complete one of the following:
   a. Answer the questions at the end of Lesson 5 in The First Communion Catechism; begin memorization of catechism questions 28-36 **or**
   b. Read Lesson 12 in *Jesus Our Life* in the Faith and Life series; review question 26 and the "Words to Know."

2. Lucia speaks of her obligation to obey the requests of the angel as well as her mother's expectation that Lucia would not lie. Of which commandments does Lucia speak? Older siblings should briefly review the Ten Commandments in Lesson 15 of *The New Saint Joseph Baltimore Catechism*. If you have not yet memorized these commandments, do so now. Review too the two great commandments as set forth by Jesus. Corresponding text paragraphs in the *CCC* include 2055, 2083, 2196; 1473, 2044, 2446-47 (418 and 436-441); 931-933, 944-945, and 1554 (435).

Wednesday, Week 4 (Day 24)

Parents: Read pages 160-170 in *The Story of a Family*.

High School and Middle School Students: Read the meditational reading on page 80.

First Communicants: Complete "Day 24" in your First Communion journal.

Family Read Aloud: Read Chapter 3 of *The Children of Fatima*.

Chapter 3—In Which Our Lady Gives the Children Another Prayer and Promises to Take Jacinta and Francisco to Heaven Soon

Comprehension Questions/Narration Prompts

1. How did the children's parents and the parish priest react when told of our Lady's visit?
2. What did Father Ferreira advise the children's mothers to do?
3. How many people were present at our Lady's visit on June 13, 1917? What was the first part of her message to the children in this visit?

Discussion Topics

1. Explain how, and why, the children's attitude toward the rosary changed. (pages 21- 22)
2. Update the outline/chart started in the last chapter to include the first part of the second visit of our Lady. Discuss how this message can be applied today.

Growing in Holiness

If the Fatima Prayer (also called the Decade Prayer) that our Lady asked the children to add after each Glory Be in the rosary has not yet been memorized, do so now. Remember to add this prayer each day when the rosary is recited. This too is an excellent prayer to be recited before the Blessed Sacrament.

Optional Catechism Lessons

1. First Communicants should complete one of the following:
    a. Write catechism questions 28-36 from *The New Saint Joseph First Communion Catechism* on index cards and review **or**
    b. In *Jesus Our Life* read Lesson 13; review the "Words to Know."
2. The children's parents held the parish priest in high regard—as a representative of Christ. Older siblings should review in Lesson 34 of *The New Saint Joseph Baltimore Catechism*, especially the section regarding Holy Orders. Corresponding text paragraphs from the *Catechism of the Catholic Church* include the following: 1142, 1548, 1551, 1563-66, 1577-78, and 1581-83 (176, 179, and 322-336).

Thursday, Week 4 (Day 25)

Parents: Read pages 170-181 in *The Story of a Family*.

High School and Middle School Students: Read the meditational reading on page 80.

First Communicants: Complete "Day 25" in your First Communion journal.

Family Read Aloud: Read Chapter 4 of *The Children of Fatima*.

Chapter 4—In Which Our Lady Continues the Message of Her Second Visit

Comprehension Questions/Narration Prompts
1. What happened when our Lady stretched out her hands toward the children?
2. What devotion did our Lady request in order to make her Heart known and loved by others? What promises did she attach to this devotion?
3. What sign allowed some of the onlookers at the second visit to believe that the lady had actually been at the holm-oak?

Discussion Topics
1. Explain what is necessary to meet the conditions of the First Five Saturdays—an offering made by us to console Mary's Immaculate Heart. How will this devotion help to make the Immaculate Heart of Mary better known and loved?
2. Summarize Lucia's definition of "reparation" on page 30. Then summarize Francisco's definition of "reparation" as found on page 31. Now compare these definitions with your answer in Chapter 2 under Discussion Topics #1 above.
3. Update the outline/chart started in the Chapter 2 to include the second part of the visit of our Lady on June 13, 1917. How can this message be applied today in your life?

Growing in Holiness
1. Begin to pray each day before the crucifix. Always make the Sign of the Cross reverently. St. Dominic often used this prayer alone to invoke God's miraculous assistance. You may use a spiritual book to help prevent distractions during your prayer time, but remember that St. Thomas Aquinas said that the finest book of all is the crucifix.
2. If you have not yet made the First Saturday Communions of Reparation, review again the requirements. Attend Mass on the first Saturday of each month for five consecutive months in addition to completing the other requirements. Try to make this a lifelong devotion even if all Saturdays are not consecutive.

Optional Catechism Lessons
1. First Communicants should complete one of the following:
   a. Write a short prayer to tell God how very much you love Him. Recite it when you are tempted to sin. Continue memorization of catechism questions 1-36 from the flash cards **or**
   b. Read Lesson 14 in *Jesus Our Life*; review "Words to Know." Ask someone to read Matthew 25:31-46 and Luke 10:29-37 to you.
2. Our Lady asked the children to "pray, to pray much." (page 34) Older siblings should read Lesson 37 in *The New Saint Joseph Baltimore Catechism* on prayer. Pertinent text paragraphs in the *Catechism of the Catholic Church* include 1235, 1671, 2157, 2559-65, 2700-2708, 2729-37 and 2752-58 (243, 245, 291, 301, 374, 534-535, and 559-577).

Friday, Week 4 (Day 26)

Parents: Read pages 182-192 in *The Story of a Family*.

High School and Middle School Students: Read the meditational reading on page 80.

First Communicants: Complete "Day 26" in your First Communion journal.

Family Read Aloud: Read Chapter 5 of *The Children of Fatima*.

Chapter 5—In Which the Children Receive Three Secrets from Our Lady and Experience a Vision of Hell

Comprehension Questions/Narration Prompts

1. How many people attended the expected third visit of our Lady to the children of Fatima on July 13, 1917? Compare this with the previous month's attendance.

2. What are the three secrets of this message from our Lady?

3. Describe how Lucia's life at home has changed since the first visit of our Lady.

Discussion Topics

1. Compare and contrast the rays that issued from our Lady's hands during the message of July 13th with those of the June 13th message.

2. Using notes from the Chapter 3 outline, compare Holy Scripture's description of hell with what the children saw during this vision. How do you think reading about hell and knowing of its existence is different from actually seeing a vision of it?

3. This chapter is entitled "A New Life." What was the new life that the children experienced after the third vision in July? Explain the change in their attitudes as well as their general spiritual conversions. (Older siblings may read text paragraph 1848 in the *Catechism of the Catholic Church*.) What can you do to imitate the children in making "little sacrifices that no one will notice"? (page 43)

4. Add the events of the third vision to your outline/chart of the Fatima apparitions and discuss their possible current application.

Growing in Holiness

The children of Fatima are now praying with joy and peace. The rays of grace given to them by the Blessed Virgin have changed their prayer lives. Ask daily for this grace. When our Lady appeared to St. Catherine Laboure of France in 1830, she spoke of the graces and blessings that flow out of the rays of her hands. But so many do not ask for these graces! Be sure to ask our Lady for the grace to want to pray, not from a sense of duty but from a true love of God and a longing to convert sinners.

Optional Catechism Lessons

1. First Communicants should complete one of the following:
   a. Complete memorization of catechism questions 1-13 and 22-36 from the First Communion Catechism; continue to review prayers **or**
   b. Review Lessons 1-14 in *Jesus Our Life* by reviewing questions 1-26 as well as the "Words to Know" from each lesson; continue to work on the memorization of the prayers at the back of the book.

2. Older siblings should study Lesson 30 on contrition in *The New Saint Joseph Baltimore Catechism* and/or read pertinent text paragraphs in the *Catechism of the Catholic Church*, which include 1451-1454 (300 and 303). Read the "Psalm of Contrition", Psalm 51; this psalm is also known as the "Miserere" or the "Prayer of Repentance."

Saturday, Week 4 and Week 5, Sunday (Days 27 and 28)

Parents: Complete reading through page 192 in *The Story of a Family*.

High School and Middle School Students: Read the meditational readings on page 80.

First Communicants: Complete an entry in your journal each day this weekend.

Family: Choose an activity in the "Weekend Projects" section of this guide.

Monday, Week 5 (Day 29)

Parents: Read pages 193-203 in *The Story of a Family.*

High School and Middle School Students: Read the meditational reading on page 81.

First Communicants: Complete "Day 29" in your First Communion journal.

Family Read Aloud: Read Chapter 6 of *The Children of Fatima.*

Chapter 6—In Which the Mayor Prevents the Children from Meeting with Our Lady

Comprehension Questions/Narration Prompts

1. Why was the mayor of Ourem upset about the events at Fatima?
2. How did Lucia react to the questions of the mayor?
3. What is the scheme of the mayor regarding the children of Fatima?

Discussion Topics

1. How would you refute the deputy's idea that religion is only a cleverly organized business that is old-fashioned and not to be tolerated in an up-to-date country? Why is religion still important in a "progressive" world?
2. What feelings, fears, and expectations do you think the three children had as they were about to be thrown into jail?

Growing in Holiness

Lucia reveals to the mayor another prayer the children had been given during the July 13th apparition: the "Sacrifice Prayer" as found on page 50 of the Windeatt biography. Memorize this prayer. Recite it often during the day as sacrifices for sinners are made. Pray that a great many sinners will be converted!

Optional Catechism Lessons

1. First Communicants should complete one of the following:
   a. In the First Communion Catechism, read Lesson 6 "The Son of God Becomes Man" and Lesson 7 "Jesus Opens Heaven for Us" **or**
   b. In *Jesus Our Life* from the Faith and Life series, read Lesson 15; review question 27. Have someone read Matthew 6: 5-15 to you.
2. Atheists are people who believe that there is no God. Older siblings should review Lesson 16 in *The New Saint Joseph Baltimore Catechism* on the first commandment as well as text paragraphs 2084-2132 (2-4 and 442-43) or the "In Brief" section 2133-41.

Tuesday, Week 5 (Day 30)

Parents: Read pages 204-214 in *The Story of a Family.*

High School and Middle School Students: Read the meditational reading on page 81.

First Communicants: Complete "Day 30" in your First Communion journal.

Family Read Aloud: Read Chapter 7 of *The Children of Fatima.*

Chapter 7—In Which the Faith and Spiritual Courage of the Children Are Tested

Comprehension Questions/Narration Prompts
1. How did the other prisoners at Ourem react to Lucia, Jacinta, and Francisco?
2. What did the mayor do on the fifth day of the children's imprisonment?
3. What did Lucia do when she thought that Jacinta and Francisco had been killed?

Discussion Topics
1. What thoughts and feelings do you think the mayor's wife might have had toward the children? What feelings do you think she may have had toward her husband?
2. All three of the children were willing to die rather than reveal the secret the lady had entrusted to them or to deny her existence. If you were in their place, what graces or assistance would you ask from heaven in order to obtain the privilege to die as a martyr for your Faith? Name some small crucifixions you can undergo each day to prepare for possible persecution or martyrdom.

Growing In Holiness
Jacinta, even in prison, prays the rosary as our Lady had requested. She prays it on her knees with her hands folded. How often do you pray on your knees in humble submission to God? Remember the importance of posture when you pray—not only with your daily rosary but also with your morning and night prayers.

Optional Catechism Lessons
1. First Communicants should complete one of the following:
    a. Answer questions at the end of Lessons 6 and 7 in *The New Saint Joseph First Communion Catechism*. Begin memorization of catechism questions 14-21 **or**
    b. Read Lesson 16 in *Jesus Our Life*. Review the "Words to Know." Have someone help you find a miracle Jesus performed in the Bible.
2. Older siblings should study Lesson 36 in *The New Saint Joseph Baltimore Catechism* on sacramentals. If desired, read text paragraphs 1667-79 (351) in the *Catechism of the Catholic Church*.

Wednesday, Week 5 (Day 31)
Parents: Read pages 215-223 in *The Story of a Family*.
High School and Middle School Students: Read the meditational reading on page 81.
First Communicants: Complete "Day 31" in your First Communion journal.
Family Read Aloud: Chapter 8 of *The Children of Fatima*.

Chapter 8—In Which the Events of August 13th Are Told, and Our Lady Makes Her August Visit

Comprehension Questions/Narration Prompts
1. Did the crowd who gathered for the lady's visit on August 13th receive a miracle as they expected?

2. Relate what happened on August 19th while the children were shepherding their sheep near the village of Valinhos.

3. What did our Lady tell Lucia to do with the gifts people were leaving at the holm-oak?

Discussion Topics

1. If you had been in attendance at the Cova on August 13th, what might your thoughts, feelings, and reactions have been concerning these events?

2. Add the information for this message to your chart on the Fatima messages as started in Chapter 2. How can you apply our Lady's message to your own life?

Growing in Holiness

Begin a family tradition of processions on feast days. Carry candles, homemade banners and/or statues. Sing hymns or pray appropriate litanies. Process either room to room in your home or throughout the neighborhood. Perhaps you can begin or end at a church. Celebrate with a special food that day. Don't forget to celebrate each member's baptismal day in this way too.

Optional Catechism Lessons

1. First Communicants should complete one of the following:
   a. Write catechism questions 14-21 from *The New Saint Joseph First Communion Catechism* on index cards and review **or**
   b. Read Lesson 17 in *Jesus Our Life*; review question 28 and the "Words to Know." If you have not memorized an Act of Contrition yet, do so now.

2. Older siblings should review Lesson 32 in *The New Saint Joseph Baltimore Catechism* on the procedure for making a good confession.

Thursday, Week 5 (Day 32)

Parents: Read pages 224-232 in *The Story of a Family*.

High School and Middle School Students: Read the meditational reading on page 82.

First Communicants: Complete "Day 32" in your First Communion journal.

Family Read Aloud: Read Chapter 9 of *The Children of Fatima*.

Chapter 9—In Which Our Lady Gives Her Fifth Message to the Children of Fatima

Comprehension Questions/Narration Prompts

1. How many people were expected for the September apparition as compared with the crowd for the August vision?

2. What was a sign that the lady was approaching?

3. Did all the people present for the fifth visit of our Lady believe that she had truly appeared?

Discussion Topics

1. You are a television reporter assigned to prepare a news report of all the events that have occurred at Fatima to date. A news report contains only facts and not opinions about any events or persons. Create a television broadcast of the Fatima events,

including a summary of the message of our Lady on September 15, 1917. Be objective but make the report as detailed as you can.

2. The apparitions at Fatima were declared "worthy of belief" by the Church in 1930. Defend the actions of the parish priest of Fatima. Why is it important that he (and us as well!) not become too involved in visions and revelations that do not have Church approval?

Growing in Holiness
Our Lady is said to be "so bright and beautiful that the sun become as nothing in her presence." (page 77) Pray the Litany of the Blessed Virgin (Litany of Loreto). Note especially the following titles appropriate to our study of our Lady of Fatima: "Gate of Heaven", "Morning Star", and "Queen of the Most Holy Rosary."

Optional Catechism Lessons
1. First Communicants should complete one of the following:
   a. Draw a picture that shows either the Christmas or the Easter story. Continue memorization of all catechism questions 1-36 from the flash cards **or**
   b. Read Lesson 18 in *Jesus Our Life*. Review question 29 and "Words to Know."
2. Father Ferreira was able to place his obligation to obedience over his curiosity; Lucia's mother took her responsibilities as a parent very seriously. Older siblings should study Lesson 19 in *The New Saint Joseph Baltimore Catechism*, especially the sections on the fourth commandment. Reflect on your obligation to obedience in imitation of the obedience of Christ. Corresponding text paragraphs on the commandments in the *Catechism of the Catholic Church* include the following: Fourth—2247-57 (455-465), Fifth—2318-30 (466-486), and Sixth—2392-2400 (487-502).

Friday, Week 5 (Day 33)
Parents: Read pages 233-243 in *The Story of a Family*.
High School and Middle School Students: Read the meditational reading on page 82.
First Communicants: Complete "Day 33" in your First Communion journal.
Family Read Aloud: Read Chapter 10 of *The Children of Fatima*.

Chapter 10—In Which the Great Miracle of the Sun Occurs

Comprehension Questions/Narration Prompts
1. How did the children of Fatima feel about the promised miracle that was to occur on October 13, 1917? How did Lucia's mother feel about it?
2. What was the mission or purpose of the messages given by our Lady of Fatima?
3. Other than the vision of the Holy Family, who did Lucia see?

Discussion Topics
1. "Faith is both a theological virtue given by God as grace, and an obligation which flows from the first commandment." (*Catechism of the Catholic Church*, Glossary) We

are all required by the first commandment to believe in God, but we are not all given the same amount of faith as a gift from God. With this in mind, defend Lucia's mother's point of view regarding the apparitions of Fatima. Try to view the visions in the light of a struggling mother who has less faith than her daughter does.

2. Summarize the message of October 13, 1917. Who did the lady say she was and what does she want? Add this information to the outline/chart begun in Chapter 2.

Growing in Holiness

The miracle of the sun caused many people to believe that the end of the world had come; they pled for mercy and made acts of contrition. Using the Ten Commandments and the beatitudes, make a sincere examination of conscience. Begin to examine your conscience each night, followed by an act of contrition. Make resolutions for the following day, choosing one sinful habit to begin to correct. If it has been more than a month since receiving the Sacrament of Penance, arrange to do so this weekend. If you do not yet have the Act of Contrition memorized, memorize one now.

Optional Catechism Lessons

1. First Communicants should complete one of the following:
   a. Complete memorization of catechism questions 1-36 from *The New Saint Joseph First Communion Catechism*, and continue to review prayers **or**
   b. As more than half the book is now complete, review Lessons 1-18 in *Jesus Our Life* by reviewing questions 1-29 as well as the "Words to Know" from each lesson. Continue to work on the memorization of the prayers at the back of the book and the Ten Commandments as needed.
2. Recitation of the rosary not only showers graces upon those who recite it, but it also builds up the spiritual treasury of the Church. Older siblings should read about temporal punishment and indulgences in Lesson 33 of *The New Saint Joseph Baltimore Catechism*. Corresponding text paragraphs in the *Catechism of the Catholic Church* include 1471-79 and 1498 (310 and 312). See also the Handbook of Indulgences, Norms and Grants for more information on indulgences as well as specific acts and prayers to which indulgences are attached.

Saturday, Week 5 and Week 6, Sunday (Days 34 and 35)

Parents: Finish any reading necessary so that you are prepared to begin on page 244 in *The Story of a Family* on Monday.

High School and Middle School Students: Read the meditational readings on page 82.

First Communicants: Complete an entry in your journal each day this weekend.

Family: Choose an activity in the "Weekend Projects" section of this guide.

Monday, Week 6 (Day 36)

Parents: Read pages 244-253 in *The Story of a Family*.

High School and Middle School Students: Read the meditational reading on pages 82-83.

First Communicants: Complete "Day 36" in your First Communion journal.

Family Read Aloud: Read Chapter 11 of *The Children of Fatima*.

Chapter 11—In Which the Children Begin to Live According to the Instructions of Our Lady

Comprehension Questions/Narration Prompts

1. From where was the miracle of the sun seen?
2. List the members of Lucia's family as mentioned on page 100.
3. How many souls did the children see in their vision of hell?

Discussion Topics

1. Summarize the activities and attitude of the atheists who went to the Cova da Iria by night. What do you think their motives were?
2. Describe the mortifications and sacrifices willingly made by Lucia, Jacinta, and Francisco. Why were they willing to make these sacrifices?
3. Discuss why an understanding of the catechism—or doctrines of our Faith—is important before receiving Holy Communion. In your opinion, what doctrines or teachings are the most important to understand before receiving this sacrament?

Growing in Holiness

Remembering that the children saw not many souls in hell but "billions and billions", renew your efforts to make sacrifices for sinners as outlined in Chapter 5. As our Lady of Fatima stated, "Penance! Penance! Penance!" Each day "offer up" some sacrifice for sinners and the holy souls of Purgatory. Especially remember to keep Friday as a day of penance. Despite some popular misconception, Fridays continue to be days of penance for Catholics. In 1966, the Catholic Bishops of the United States removed the requirement of abstinence from meat on Fridays (except during Lent). Their reasoning was that abstaining from meat may not be the best means of practicing penance. At this same time, the bishops gave each of us the responsibility of disciplining ourselves with another more meaningful form of fasting and penance. Just as you keep Sunday a day of celebration in remembrance of Christ's resurrection, make Friday a day of penance in remembrance of His sacrifice for you.

Optional Catechism Lessons

1. First Communicants should complete one of the following:
    a. Read Lesson 8 in *The New Saint Joseph First Communion Catechism* **or**
    b. In *Jesus Our Life* read Lesson 19; review the "Words to Know" as well as the "Steps for the Sacrament of Confession."
2. Atheists believe there is no God and do not believe in life after death. Older siblings should study the Church's teaching of God and His perfections in Lesson 2 of *The*

New Saint Joseph Baltimore Catechism. Read text paragraphs 268-78, 312-14, 31-55, 65-75, 80-83, and 134-41 (41-43 and 50-56) in the *Catechism of the Catholic Church*.

Tuesday, Week 6 (Day 37)

Parents: Read pages 253-261 in *The Story of a Family*.
High School and Middle School Students: Read the meditational reading on page 83.
First Communicants: Complete "Day 37" in your First Communion journal.
Family Read Aloud: Read Chapter 12 of *The Children of Fatima*.

Chapter 12—In Which the Children Attend School, and Francisco Receives His First Holy Communion

Comprehension Questions/Narration Prompts
1. Despite the staring and whispering of the other children, why did the three children want to stay in school?
2. When did the Blessed Virgin appear again to Jacinta and Francisco and what did she say?
3. What was the one thing that troubled Francisco as he neared death?

Discussion Topics
1. Describe the difference in Francisco's attitude toward the Church, the rosary, visits to the Blessed Sacrament, etc. What made his attitude change?
2. Review Jacinta's thoughts on page 115 regarding the Will of God. With these thoughts in mind, compose a prayer that will strengthen you and allow you to begin to live in God's Will.

Growing in Holiness
Francisco no longer feels that the rosary is a tiresome repetition of prayers. Now with his soul's eye, he views the mysteries as pictures of the life of our Lord or the Blessed Virgin. Many rosary meditation books contain pictures to illustrate each mystery. Purchase or borrow several of these to enrich your rosary recitation. (Fr. Lovasik wrote the children's rosary booklet, "The Holy Rosary", which contains both pictures and short meditations. The Mary Fabyan Windeatt coloring book about the rosary will allow you to color your own pictures, or you may draw your own series of pictures to accompany your meditation.) Re-read Francisco's method of meditation described on pages 111-12. Try to incorporate this method into your daily rosary.

Optional Catechism Lessons
1. First Communicants should complete one of the following:
    a. Answer the questions at the end of Lesson 8 in *The New Saint Joseph First Communion Catechism*; begin memorization of catechism questions 37-43 **or**
    b. If *The New Saint Joseph Baltimore Catechism* is available to you, review Lesson 32 on "How to Make a Good Confession." If it is not available, try to find a story in the Bible that shows God's forgiveness and mercy.

2. ". . . their only trips to the village church had been on Sundays and feast days to attend Mass." (page 109) Older siblings should review Lesson 18 in *The New Saint Joseph Baltimore Catechism*. Corresponding text paragraphs in the *Catechism of the Catholic Church* include the following: 2142-59 (447-449)—or the "In Brief" section 2160-67—and 2168-88—or the "In Brief" section 2189-95 (450-454).

Wednesday, Week 6 (Day 38)

Parents: Read pages 262-275 in *The Story of a Family*.

High School and Middle School Students: Read the meditational reading on page 83.

First Communicants: Complete "Day 38" in your First Communion journal.

Family Read Aloud: Read Chapter 13 of *The Children of Fatima*.

Chapter 13—In Which Jacinta's Suffering Increases

Comprehension Questions/Narration Prompts

1. On what day did Francisco Martos die?
2. In whose keeping has Our Lord entrusted the peace of the world?

Discussion Topics

1. "Ever since our Lady's third visit, Jacinta had grown in the grace of loving souls." (page 126) Recall the events of our Lady's third visit. Describe in your own words what the "grace of loving souls" is. How does Jacinta demonstrate that grace? How can you demonstrate that grace?
2. Relate the great sacrifice of Lucia, as she would describe it. In your opinion, is her sacrifice greater than the sufferings of Jacinta? Why or why not?

Growing in Holiness

Note the change in the Sacrifice Prayer—an additional petition praying for the pope (page 129)—added after Jacinta had a vision of the pope with his head in his hands, weeping.

Two other prayers are offered in this chapter: "My God, I love You because of the graces which You have given me", and "Sweet Heart of Mary, be my salvation." Lucia began praying the first prayer after talking with Rev. Dr. Formigao, her first spiritual director. Father Cruz from Lisbon taught them the second prayer. Jacinta said it often. Memorize both of these prayers. Pray them often.

Optional Catechism Lessons

1. First Communicants should complete one of the following:
    a. Write catechism questions 37-43 from *The New Saint Joseph First Communion Catechism* on index cards and review **or**
    b. In *Jesus Our Life*, read Lesson 20. Read Luke 19:1-10, the story of Zacchaeus.
2. Older siblings should review Lesson 9 in *The New Saint Joseph Baltimore Catechism* on the Holy Spirit and grace. Corresponding text paragraphs in the *CCC* include 683-86, 691-93, 733-36 (136-138 and 144-146); 1996-2000, 2003, and 2021-2024 (423-425).

Thursday, Week 6 (Day 39)

Parents: Read pages 275-286 in *The Story of a Family*.

High School and Middle School Students: Read the meditational reading on page 84.

First Communicants: Complete "Day 39" in your First Communion journal.

Family Read Aloud: Read Chapter 14 of *The Children of Fatima*.

Chapter 14—In Which We Learn of Jacinta's Love for Sinners as She Continues to Suffer and Make Sacrifices

Comprehension Questions/Narration Prompts

1. Why did Jacinta go to Ourem? What was the result?
2. When and why did Jacinta go to Lisbon?
3. What two privileges did Jacinta describe as "heaven on earth"? (page 137)
4. What was Jacinta's last sacrifice?

Discussion Topics

1. Summarize the Blessed Virgin Mary's comments to Jacinta during her various visits to Jacinta at the orphanage. Include her comments on war, sin, chastity, the priesthood, and governments. How relevant today are these concerns of our Lady?

2. Expand on these comments made by Jacinta as recorded by Mother Godinho at the Lisbon orphanage: "More souls go to Hell because of sins of the flesh than for any other reason." "Many marriages are not good; they do not please Our Lord and are not of God!" "People are lost because they do not think of the death of Our Lord and do not do penance." "If men only knew what eternity is, they would do everything in their power to change their lives."

Growing in Holiness

"The sins which cause most people to go to hell are the sins against purity." (page 139) Examine different aspects of your life—music, movies, television, dress, reading material, companions, etc. to determine what adjustments may be needed in your entertainment, bedroom décor, or clothing style. Remember that sin first takes place in your thoughts; post your angel there to help protect you from sin. Pray often "Come, Holy Spirit, come" for the strength and perseverance to live a pure life.

Optional Catechism Lessons

1. First Communicants should complete one of the following:
    a. Draw a picture of yourself as a soldier of Christ. What will your weapons be? Name the seven sacraments. Continue memorization of catechism questions 1-43 from the flash cards **or**
    b. In *Jesus Our Life*, read Lesson 21; review the "Words to Know." Have someone read to you the following passages from the Bible regarding the Good Shepherd: Luke 15:1-7 and John 10:1-15.

2. Review the commandments in Lesson 20 of *The New Saint Joseph Baltimore Catechism*, especially the ninth commandment. Additional information on the commandments can be found in text paragraphs 2401-2557 of the *Catechism of the Catholic Church* or the "In Brief" sections as follows: Seventh—2450-63 (503-520), Eighth—2504-2513 (521-526), Ninth—2528-2533 (527-530), and Tenth—2551-57 (531-533).

Friday, Week 6 (Day 40)

Parents: Read pages 286-295 in *The Story of a Family.*
High School and Middle School Students: Read the meditational reading on page 84.
First Communicants: Complete "Day 40" in your First Communion journal.
Family Read Aloud: Read Chapter 15 of *The Children of Fatima.*

Chapter 15—In Which Lucia Leaves Fatima

Comprehension Questions/Narration Prompts
1. When did Jacinta die and where was she originally buried?
2. After the death of Jacinta, what other trial did Lucia undergo?
3. Where did Lucia go in the spring of 1921 and why?
4. What was to be Lucia's new name?

Discussion Topics
1. In your own words, summarize the Fatima messages; use the partial summary of the Fatima message given at the bottom of page 155 as well as the outline/chart compiled by you throughout this study guide.
2. Imagine leaving home at the age of fourteen. What might your thoughts and feelings be? What places, people, and activities would you miss?

Growing in Holiness
"Somehow the various visits with our Lady, the many prayers and sacrifices she had made for sinners during the past four years, had disposed her soul for the great grace of being completely abandoned to God's Will." (page 150) "Because once again she had asked for and been given the grace to do not her will, but the Will of God." (page 152) Abandon yourself to the Will of God. Remember that God is with each of us each moment—loving, leading, calling. The time to surrender is now. Begin to practice the presence of God. Do you will what God wills?

Optional Catechism Lessons
1. First Communicants should complete one of the following:
    a. Complete memorization of catechism questions 37-43 from Lesson 8 in *The New Saint Joseph First Communion Catechism* and continue to work on the prayers **or**
    b. Review Lessons 1-21 in *Jesus Our Life* by reviewing questions 1-29 as well as the "Words to Know" from each lesson; continue memory work on the prayers contained at the back of the book as needed

2. Baron d'Alvayazer believed that great graces would be showered upon his family if he honored the body of Jacinta. (page 144) Older siblings should review Lesson 17 in *The New Saint Joseph Baltimore Catechism* on honoring saints, relics, and images. The corresponding text paragraphs in the *CCC* include 828, 1195, 2683 (165, 242, 294, 429, 564), and 1159-62 (240).

Saturday, Week 6 and Week 7, Sunday (Days 41 and 42)

Parents: Finish any reading necessary so that you are prepared to begin on page 296 in *The Story of a Family* on Monday.

High School and Middle School Students: Read the meditational readings on pages 84-85.

First Communicants: Complete an entry in your journal each day this weekend.

Family: Choose an activity in the "Weekend Projects" section of this guide.

Monday, Week 7 (Day 43)

Parents: Read pages 296-304 in *The Story of a Family*.

High School and Middle School Students: Read the meditational reading on page 85.

First Communicants: Complete "Day 43" in your First Communion journal.

Family Read Aloud: Read Chapter 1 of *The Patron Saint of First Communicants, The Story of Blessed Imelda Lambertini* by Mary Fabyan Windeatt.

Chapter 1—In Which Imelda Is Born

Comprehension Questions/Narration Prompts
1. Where and when does this story take place?
2. What does Peter feel brought John, the baker's son, back home?
3. Why does Peter start out to see Donna Castora?
4. Why were the castle bells ringing?

Discussion Topics
1. Describe in detail a "face strongly marked with the peace of Christ." (page 3) From what is known thus far about Peter, tell some things he does to obtain this peace. What can you do to have the peace of Christ shine from your face?
2. "Sorrow, bravely borne, is nothing more than a key to the wonders of heaven." (page 5) Explain what this means.

Growing in Holiness
Peter and John talk about how many of us fail to thank God for His countless blessings. Our prayers of petition are ardently recited, but we oftentimes forget to thank God for granting our requests. Remember to thank God each day for His many blessings. If possible, go each day—if only for several minutes—to thank Him before the Blessed Sacrament. Spend extra time after receiving Holy Communion to thank God for the great gift of His Son.

Remember the great gift Jesus has given us—the gift of Himself. He is truly present in every tabernacle of every Catholic Church. Be sure to acknowledge His Presence when you walk or drive by a Catholic Church—pray the Sign of the Cross and say a short prayer such as "My Jesus, I believe that You are present in the most Blessed Sacrament." He waits there for you—the uncaptured Prisoner.

Optional Catechism Lessons
1. First Communicants should complete one of the following:
   a. In *The New Saint Joseph First Communion Catechism*, read Lesson 9 **or**
   b. In *Jesus Our Life* from the Faith and Life series, read Lesson 22; review questions 30-31, and the "Words to Know."
2. This chapter's title, "A Child Is Born", could also be the title of the first two chapters of Luke. Read Luke 1:26-38 and Luke 2:1-20. Review Lesson 7 in *The New Saint Joseph Baltimore Catechism*. Corresponding text paragraphs in the *CCC* include 359, 423, 461-463, 479-483, and 525-34 (67, 79, 85-86, 89-92, and 103).

Tuesday, Week 7 (Day 44)

Parents: Read pages 304-315 in *The Story of a Family*.

High School and Middle School Students: Read the meditational reading on page 85.

First Communicants: Complete "Day 44" in your First Communion journal.

Family Read Aloud: Read Chapter 2 of *The Patron Saint of First Communicants*.

Chapter 2—In Which Donna Castora Dreams of St. Dominic

Comprehension Questions/Narration Prompts

1. How did the Lambertini's celebrate the birth of their daughter?
2. What was Donna Castora's dream and what did she feel it meant?
3. What did Donna Castora's brother, the archbishop, advise about the dream?

Discussion Topics

1. Describe the dream Donna Castora had as she rested after the birth of her daughter.
2. Find examples of the five forms of prayer—blessing and adoration, petition, intercession, thanksgiving, and praise within the first two chapters of this book. How can you use each form today in your prayers?

Growing in Holiness

"Every child born into the world is given the grace to become a saint. Castora, you must teach little Imelda this truth and help her to use the graces God gives her." (page 21) Pray daily for more graces to persevere in the spiritual life. Be aware each moment of the graces and opportunities for grace that God offers you. Receive Holy Communion as often as possible.

Optional Catechism Lessons

1. First Communicants should complete one of the following:
    a. Answer the questions from Lesson 9 in *The New Saint Joseph First Communion Catechism*; begin memorization of questions 44-45 **or**
    b. Read Lesson 23 in *Jesus Our Life* from the Faith and Life series; review question 32 and the "Words to Know."
2. Donna Castora's brother, an archbishop and successor of the Apostles, was to perform Imelda's baptism. Older siblings should review Lesson 12 in *The New Saint Joseph Baltimore Catechism*, which explains the marks of the Church. Corresponding text paragraphs in the *Catechism of the Catholic Church* include 811-15, 823-31, 846-48, and 857-62, or the "In Brief" section 866-70 (161-63, 165-68, and 174).

Wednesday, Week 7 (Day 45)

Parents: Read pages 315-322 in *The Story of a Family*.

High School and Middle School Students: Read the meditational reading on page 85.

First Communicants: Complete "Day 45" in your First Communion journal.

Family Read Aloud: Read Chapter 3 of *The Patron Saint of First Communicants*.

Chapter 3—In Which Imelda Longs for Our Lord

Comprehension Questions/Narration Prompts
1. What are some of the gifts that God had bestowed upon Imelda?
2. What did Imelda want as a present for her fifth birthday? Why was she not to get it?
3. What was Imelda's favorite gift of all the presents received?

Discussion Topics
1. Explain Imelda's idea that all people in the state of grace are a tabernacle. On what doctrines does she base this idea? How did this thought affect her daily life? How can it affect yours? (See 1 Corinthians 3:16 and Galatians 2:20.)
2. Why would Imelda's parents be grateful for the interruption of Beatrice? (page 31) What might you say to Imelda to explain the delay necessary for her to receive our Lord in Holy Communion? What might you say to console her?

Growing in Holiness
Imelda was the daughter of very wealthy parents. Notice her plush surroundings and lavish gifts. (pages 26 and 27) Yet her favorite birthday gift was a rosary given to her by her mother. With all the extravagance around her, she still put much importance on Godly things. Re-evaluate your priorities. What are your feelings about presents? What value do you place on religious or spiritual gifts? Where do you spend your money and your time? Are you trying to accumulate worldly possessions or heavenly treasures? What adjustments do you need to make in your life in order to imitate Imelda more closely?

Optional Catechism Lessons
1. First Communicants should complete one of the following:
    a. Write catechism questions 44-45 from *The New Saint Joseph First Communion Catechism* on index cards and review **or**
    b. Read Lesson 24 in *Jesus Our Life*. Review question 33 and the "Words to Know."
2. Read Lesson 26 in *The New Saint Joseph Baltimore Catechism* on the Holy Eucharist as well as corresponding text paragraphs 1322-44 (271-76) in the *CCC*.

Thursday, Week 7 (Day 46)
Parents: Read pages 323-331 in *The Story of a Family*.
High School and Middle School Students: Read the meditational reading on page 85.
First Communicants: Complete "Day 46" in your First Communion journal.
Family Read Aloud: Read Chapter 4 of *The Patron Saint of First Communicants*.

Chapter 4—In Which Imelda Shares Her Knowledge of the Dominican Order

Comprehension Questions/Narration Prompts
1. Who were Imelda's imaginary companions?
2. What was Imelda's attitude toward the required wait for Holy Communion?
3. Why was Beatrice uneasy over Imelda's account of the Dominican saints?
4. What was Imelda's daily prayer for her friend Peter, the basket-maker?

5. List the two wishes Imelda expresses while visiting the Convent of St. Agnes.

Discussion Topics

1. In your own words, relate the story of the founding of the Dominican Order, especially its history in Bologna, Italy. Include such people as St. Dominic, Father Reginald, and Blessed Diana d'Andalo.
2. Re-read Imelda's explanation of the purpose of a cloistered life on page 46. Briefly summarize each sentence of the first paragraph on that page. Name at least two ways that each of these things can be demonstrated and/or accomplished.

Growing in Holiness

Imelda had great trust in God's care for her: "The best thing to do was to bear the disappointment bravely and trust that He would let everything turn to good." (page 37) Think about the last disappointment you had. What was your attitude? What do you think you could do differently in order to mimic more closely the attitude of Imelda? How disappointed are you when you are unable to receive Holy Communion?

Optional Catechism Lessons

1. First Communicants should complete one of the following:
   a. Spend some time in front of a crucifix meditating upon the sufferings of Jesus. If possible, go to your parish church to meditate before the crucifix there or to pray the Stations of the Cross. Continue memorization of catechism questions 1-45 from the flash cards or
   b. Read Lesson 25 in *Jesus Our Life*; review questions 34-35 and the "Words to Know."
2. Review Lesson 13 in *The New Saint Joseph Baltimore Catechism* on the communion of saints. Corresponding text paragraphs in the *CCC* include the following: 946-948, 950, 954-962, 1055, 1331, 1474-1477, and 2635 (195-96 and 211).

Friday, Week 7 (Day 47)

Parents: Read pages 332-341 in *The Story of a Family*.
High School and Middle School Students: Read the meditational reading on page 86.
First Communicants: Complete "Day 47" in your First Communion journal.
Family Read Aloud: Read Chapter 5 of *The Patron Saint of First Communicants*.

Chapter 5—In Which Imelda Joins the Convent of St. Mary Magdalen

Comprehension Questions/Narration Prompts

1. What convent did Imelda enter as a religious? How old was she?
2. As she gave herself to God and received the habit, for what did she ask?
3. List some of the virtues Imelda was expected to acquire as a novice.
4. What was Imelda's new duty in the convent?

Discussion Topics

1. What types of mixed emotions might Imelda's parents experience on the day their daughter entered the convent of the Sisters of Mary Magdalen? Do you think both parents would have the same reactions to this event?

2. List some of the ways in which Imelda failed as a novice. Describe the procedure of the convent in dealing with these faults. If this procedure were to be enacted in your house, how would you and other family members react?

Growing in Holiness

"Peter, I do pray for you," she said gently. "Every day. You know that. But I fear I can never pray for you or anyone as I really wish." (page 58) And "When will they let me pray for people as I really want to pray?" (page 58) Imelda is crying out to receive Holy Communion so that she may pray for people in a better way—with the Lord in her heart. Remember each time you receive the Eucharist to ask that the graces obtained with reception be applied to specific intentions. This can be done for each act you do— each prayer you make—but the graces of the Eucharist are infinite whereas the graces we can obtain for the recitation of the rosary, for example, are limited. Remember each loved one, each "cause" (peace in our world, an end to abortion, etc.), your own spiritual needs, the intentions of the Holy Father, and those for whom you have promised to pray. Ask your guardian angel to help you remember those you have promised to pray for—or to have your angel offer those intentions in prayer for you.

Optional Catechism Lessons

1. First Communicants should complete one of the following:
   a. Do a complete review of catechism questions 1-45 in *The New Saint Joseph First Communion Catechism*; work on prayers as needed **or**
   b. Review all the questions studied thus far (1-35) in *Jesus Our Life*. Also review the "Words to Know" from each lesson; continue memory work on the prayers contained at the back of the book as needed.

2. "For years after their marriage they had waited for God to send her (Imelda) to them." (page 50) Read about the Sacrament of Matrimony as well as the purpose of marriage in Lesson 35 in *The New Saint Joseph Baltimore Catechism* and text paragraphs 1601, 1614-17, 1625-30, 1638-42, and 1652-58 (337 and 341-350) or the "In Brief" section 1659-66 of the *Catechism of the Catholic Church*.

Saturday, Week 7 and Week 8, Sunday (Days 48 and 49)

Parents: Finish any reading necessary so that you are prepared to begin on page 341 in *The Story of a Family* on Monday.

High School and Middle School Students: Read the meditational readings on page 86.

First Communicants: Complete an entry in your journal each day this weekend.

Family: Choose an activity in the "Weekend Projects" section of this guide.

Monday, Week 8 (Day 50)

Parents: Read pages 341-351 in *The Story of a Family*.

High School and Middle School Students: Read the meditational reading on page 87.

First Communicants: Complete "Day 50" in your First Communion journal.

Family Read Aloud: Read Chapter 6 in *The Patron Saint of First Communicants*.

Chapter 6—In Which Our Lord Comes to Imelda in an Unexpected Way

Comprehension Questions/Narration Prompts

1. What was preventing Imelda from receiving Communion at the age of eleven?
2. What did Imelda state as the requirements for receiving Holy Communion? (page 64)
3. What reason did the nuns give for Imelda's tears after Mass on the vigil of the feast of Ascension? What was the real reason for her tears?
4. What is "The Miracle" of this chapter?

Discussion Topics

1. The mission of the Dominicans is to preach and teach. Re-read Ms. Windeatt's explanation of their mission on pages 62 and 63. Describe specifically what Dominicans do.
2. Explain what it means to be a missionary. What can you do to become a missionary and save souls for Christ?

Growing in Holiness

Our Lord came to Imelda in a miraculous way. Remember that each time He comes to us in Holy Communion, it too is a miracle. Common bread and wine become the Body, Blood, Soul, and Divinity of Jesus Christ. Jesus, the second Person of the Blessed Trinity, becomes physically present in each of us. As the Trinity is three Persons in one God, we also receive God the Father and God the Holy Spirit in each Communion. Never forget or grow accustomed to this awesome fact! If we all truly knew and understood this in our minds and hearts, would we ever get off our knees after Holy Communion?

Optional Catechism Lessons

1. First Communicants should complete one of the following:
   a. In the *The New Saint Joseph First Communion Catechism*, read Lesson 10 or
   b. In *Jesus Our Life* from the Faith and Life series, read Lesson 26; review the parts of the Mass as well as the articles used at Mass
2. To preach and to teach is the mission of the Dominican order. The mission of the Church is to "teach, sanctify, and rule the faithful in the name of Christ." Review Lesson 11 in *The New Saint Joseph Baltimore Catechism*. Read corresponding text paragraphs in the *Catechism of the Catholic Church*: 77, 688, 749-60, 763-80, 857-62, 880-96, 1555-56, and 1562 (147-152 and 182-191).

Tuesday, Week 8 (Day 51)

Parents: Read pages 351-362 in *The Story of a Family*.

High School and Middle School Students: Read the meditational reading on page 87.

First Communicants: Complete "Day 51" in your First Communion journal.

Family Read Aloud: Read Chapter 7 in *The Patron Saint of First Communicants*.

Chapter 7—In Which Imelda's Dream Comes True

Comprehension Questions/Narration Prompts

1. How long did the nuns remain in thanksgiving after the miracle of the floating Host?
2. After seeing Imelda, how did the Prioress describe Holy Communion?
3. What was the reaction of Imelda's parents when they learned of her death?
4. What was the first miracle attributed to Imelda's intercession after her death?

Discussion Topics

1. Discuss how the Prioress and the chaplain would describe the miraculous event of Imelda's first Holy Communion. How might their reactions and perceptions be different?
2. In your opinion, which miracle—the miracle of Imelda's first Holy Communion or the miracle of Peter's restored sight—was the greater miracle? Support your argument with quotations from the book, Scripture, or Catholic doctrine.

Growing in Holiness

"We can only love what we know . . . and so we ought to do all we can to know God. Then it will be very easy to love Him and to do His Will." (pages 76-77) Spend more time in front of a crucifix and in front of the Blessed Sacrament meditating on God's great love for you. When we spend more time with someone we love, our love increases. And with our human nature, we more easily love Someone when we realize how much He loves us. Be sure to mediate on Jesus' great love for you after receiving Him in Holy Communion. As the structure of the Mass does not allow an adequate thanksgiving to be made before Mass is completed, remain in thanksgiving after Mass for several minutes. Remember that the nuns in this chapter remained in humble thanksgiving for over an hour.

The following prayer of Blessed Padre Pio can be recited after receiving Communion:

Stay with me, Lord, for it is necessary to have You present so that I do not forget You. You know how easily I abandon You. Stay with me, Lord, because I am weak and I need Your strength, that I may not fall so often. Stay with me, Lord, for You are my life, and without You, I am without fervor. Stay with me, Lord, for You are my light, and without You, I am in darkness. Stay with me, Lord, to show me Your will. Stay with me, Lord, so that I hear Your voice and follow You. Stay with me, Lord, for I desire to love You very much, and always be in Your company. Stay with me, Lord, if You wish me to be faithful to You. Stay with me, Lord, for as poor as my soul is, I wish it to be a place of consolation for You, a nest of love. Stay with me, Jesus, for it is getting late and the day is coming to a close, and life passes, death, judgment, and eternity approach. It is necessary to renew my strength, so that I will not stop along the way and for that, I need You. It is getting late and death approaches. I fear the darkness, the temptations, the dryness, the cross, the sorrows. Oh how I need You, dear Jesus, in this night of exile! Stay with me tonight, Jesus, in life with all its dangers, I need You. Let me recognize You as Your disciples did at the breaking of the bread, so that the Eucharistic Communion be the light which disperses the darkness, the force which sustains me, the unique joy of my heart. Stay with me, Lord because at the hour of my death, I want to remain united to You, if not by Communion, at least by grace and love. Stay with me, Jesus. I do not ask for divine consolation, because I do not merit it, but the gift of Your Presence. Oh yes, I ask this of You! Stay with me, Lord, for it is You alone I look for, Your love, Your grace, Your will, Your Heart, Your spirit, because I love You and ask no other reward but to love You more and more. With a firm love, I will love You with all my heart while on earth and continue to love You perfectly during all eternity. Amen.

Optional Catechism Lessons
1. First Communicants should complete one of the following:
    a. Answer questions at the end of Lesson 10 in the First Communion Catechism; begin memorization of catechism questions 46-47 or
    b. Read Lesson 27 in *Jesus Our Life*. Review question 36 and "Words to Know."
2. Ms. Windeatt speaks of Imelda "reaching Paradise." (page 79) In addition to its reference to heaven, Paradise is also the name of the garden in which Adam and Eve lived before they sinned. Review Lesson 5 in *The New Saint Joseph Baltimore Catechism* on creation and the fall of man. Corresponding text paragraphs in the *Catechism of the Catholic Church* include 355-58, 362-68, 375, 396-412—or the "In Brief" section 416-421—490-93 and 2177 (66-78).

Wednesday, Week 8 (Day 52)

Parents: Read pages 362-374 in *The Story of a Family*.

High School and Middle School Students: Begin to read the parables of Jesus as outlined on page 87.

First Communicants: Complete "Day 52" in your First Communion journal.

Family Read Aloud: Read Chapters 1 and 2 in *The King of the Golden City, An Allegory for Children* by Mother Mary Loyola.

Note: *The King of the Golden City, An Allegory for Children*, originally published in 1921, was written by Mother Mary Loyola of the Bar Convent in York, England, in response to a student's request for instructions along with "little stories" to help her prepare for First Holy Communion. An allegory is a story or narrative in which a moral principle or truth is presented by use of fictional characters or events. In an allegory characters, objects, and events usually symbolize something else. By figuring out what they symbolize or parallel, the lesson the story is intended to teach can be determined. Jesus often taught moral lessons by making using of parables—a teaching tool very similar to an allegory. Older siblings have the option of adding a study of Jesus' parables in conjunction with the oral reading of this book. The "Carmelite Connections" section also allows older readers to develop a deeper prayer life by meditating on the writings of several Carmelite saints.

Parallel Figures Chart
CHAPTER 1: the King, the Golden City, the country of the travelers (Land of Exile), the rebel lord Malignus, the Happy Ones, the maid, the maid's hut, the wildflowers, the King's simple robe of white, the quarter of an hour spent within the hut together, the path to the hut, the wounds of the King, the unclean hut, no fit spot to lay them (the King's gifts) down
CHAPTER 2: lieutenants, prince of the Court (Prince Guardian), teachers

Discussion Topics
1. Discuss the relationship between the little maid and Jesus when they were meeting in the woods with their relationship after Jesus had come to her hut. How was it different when she began to take His coming to her hut for granted? Why is it important to always prepare ourselves for His Communion with us? How can we use the idea of the decoration of flowers in anticipation of His coming to help us? (For more information, see pages vi-viii of this manual.)
2. What must we do to be crowned by Jesus in death? Why do you think He gives us other teachers rather than teaching and leading us all directly? Is it easier to obey Jesus directly or His teachers? Why? What has He done to make our union with Him in the Golden City easier?

Searching Scripture
Chapter 1: Matthew 11:28-30, Hebrews 11:13-16 and Hebrews 13:14
Chapter 2: Exodus 20:1-17, John 14:15, and 1 Corinthians 9:24-27

Growing in Holiness
CHAPTER 1: Make sure that you adequately prepare for Jesus' coming to you in each Holy Communion. Do not ever take this great Gift for granted! Be mindful of distractions during both your preparation time and your thanksgiving time. Be sure to spend time after each Communion in thanksgiving. Note that each time Jesus comes to the little maid in her hut, He stays with her for a quarter of an hour. The Church teaches that the physical presence of Jesus remains with each of us for ten to twenty minutes before the Host is completely ingested into our bodies. Be aware of this physical presence when you receive Him in Holy Communion. Use this time for thanksgiving and prayer.
CHAPTER 2: Remember that those in authority over you are representatives of Jesus Himself. Treat the direction and instruction received from priests and your parents as coming directly from Jesus.

Carmelite Connections

CHAPTER 1:

1. ". . . mental prayer, in my view, is nothing but friendly intercourse, and frequent solitary converse, with Him Who we know loves us." (*Life of the Holy Mother Teresa of Jesus* VIII.5)

2. "A fine humility it would be if I had the Emperor of Heaven and earth in my house, coming to it to do me a favor and to delight in my company, and I were so humble that I would not answer His questions, nor remain with Him, nor accept what He gave me, but left Him alone." (*Way of Perfection* XXVIII.3)

3. ". . . until the accidents of bread have been consumed by our natural heat, the good Jesus is with us and we should not lose so good an opportunity but should come to Him. If, while He went about in the world, the sick were healed merely by touching His clothes, how can we doubt that He will work miracles when He is within us, if we have faith, or that He will give us what we ask of Him since he is in our house? His Majesty is not wont to offer us too little payment for His lodging if we treat Him well." (*Way of Perfection* XXXIV.9)

4. "Imagine that this Lord Himself is at your side and see how lovingly and how humbly He is teaching you—and, believe me, you should stay with so good a Friend for as long as you can before you leave Him. If you become accustomed to having Him at your side, and if He sees that you love Him to be there and are always trying to please Him, you will never be able, as we put it, to send Him away, nor will He ever fail you. He will help you in all your trials; you will have Him everywhere. Do you think it is a small thing to have such a Friend as that beside you?" (*Way of Perfection* XXVI.1)

5. "If I had understood then, as I do now, how this great King *really* dwells within this little palace of my soul, I should not have left Him alone so often, but should have stayed with Him and never have allowed His dwelling-place to get so dirty. How wonderful it is that He, Whose greatness could fill a thousand worlds, and very many more, should confine Himself within so small a space." (*Way of Perfection* XXVIII.12)

As we first come to know the little maid, she is just beginning her journey toward the Golden City. She shows us some characteristics of the classical first stage—the purgative way—of perfection in the Christian life: a growing desire to travel the road toward perfection, the continual struggle against sin and temptation, increased interest in prayer, and the longing to atone for past sins.

CHAPTER 2:

1. "Our Lord has no need of books or teachers to instruct our souls. He, the Teacher of Teachers, instructs us without any noise of words. I have never heard Him speak, yet I know He is within me. He is there, always guiding and inspiring me; and just when I need them, lights, hitherto unseen, break in." (*Story of a Soul*, Chapter VIII)

2. "Humility must always be doing its work like the bee making its honey in the hive; without humility all will be lost. Still, we should remember that the bee is constantly flying about from flower to flower, and in the same way, believe me, the soul must

sometimes emerge from self-knowledge and soar aloft in meditation upon the great-ness and the majesty of its God. Doing this will help it to realize its own baseness better than thinking of it own nature, and it will be freer from the reptiles which en-ter the first rooms—that is, the rooms of self-knowledge. For although, as I say, it is through the abundant mercy of God that the soul studies to know itself, yet one can have too much of a good thing, as the saying goes, and believe me, we shall reach much greater heights of virtue by thinking upon the virtue of God than if we stay in our own little plot of ground and tie ourselves down to it completely." (*Interior Castle* I.ii.8)

Dilecta continues to proceed through the purgative way of perfection. When we com-pare Dilecta's present condition with the traits of St. Teresa of Avila's seven mansions, we see that she has entered the castle through prayer and has several characteristics of the first mansions: an earnest, continual effort to avoid sin; a desire to avoid offending God; and imperfect progress due to her attachment to self and her desires. She is still absorbed in worldly matters but is beginning to turn from the worldly life to a life cen-tered on the Trinity.

Holy Scripture speaks of this first Teresian mansion in Titus 2:11-14: "For the grace of God has appeared, saving all and training us to reject godless ways and worldly desires and to live temperately, justly, and devoutly in this age, as we await the blessed hope, the appearance of the glory of the great God and of our savior Jesus Christ, who gave Himself for us to deliver us from all lawlessness and to cleanse for himself a people as his own, eager to do what is good."

Optional Catechism Lessons
1. First Communicants should complete one of the following:
    a. Write catechism questions 46-47 from *The New Saint Joseph First Communion Catechism* on index cards and review **or**
    b. Read Lesson 28 in *Jesus Our Life* from the Faith and Life series; review ques-tion 37 and the prayers suggested before and after Holy Communion.
2. Each of the following lessons will list several words or doctrines of faith from *The New Saint Joseph Baltimore Catechism*—both No. 1 and No. 2—which will serve not only as review of the lessons previously studied by older siblings but also as an illustration of their practical application. Use the "Dictionary and Index" found at the end of the catechism for ease in location. An attempt should also be made to locate its refer-ence or symbol in *The King of the Golden City*: CHAPTER 1: heaven, devil, grace, and penance; CHAPTER 2: Redemption, Ten Commandments (commandments), How to gain the happiness of heaven (Questions #3 and #4), and obedience (obey)

Thursday, Week 8 (Day 53)
Parents: Read pages 375-383 in *The Story of a Family*.
High School and Middle School Students: Read the parables outlined on page 87.
First Communicants: Complete "Day 53" in your First Communion journal.
Family Read Aloud: Read Chapters 3 and 4 in *The King of the Golden City*.

Narration
After reading, narrate the events of each chapter.

Parallel Figures Chart
CHAPTER 3: signs, the straight road
CHAPTER 4: a large House, the School, the Gymnasium, the Armory, the Hospital or Infirmary, the Banquet Hall, the Royal Audience Chamber

Discussion Topics
1. What is the purpose of the commandments of God, the laws of the Church, the ideals of the beatitudes and the examples of the saints? Why are we happier when we are obedient to them? Why are we happier when we submit ourselves to the example of Christ and fight our own natural tendency toward sin? What has God given us to make this battle against our own wills easier?
2. Outline each of the seven sacraments stating the purpose each performs in helping us on our journey toward heaven. Is one more important than the others are? If so, which one? Other than the sacraments, what else has God provided to assist us in obtaining our heavenly reward?

Searching Scripture
CHAPTER 3: Psalm 84, Isaiah 35:8-10, and 1 Peter 2:11
CHAPTER 4: John 14:2, Romans 8:14-17, and 1 Corinthians 2:9

Growing in Holiness
CHAPTER 3: Practice saying "no" to yourself by making little sacrifices each day in order to strengthen your will. Every day do at least one thing that you do not want to do. Always remember that you are on a journey; life here on earth is temporary. Our real home is not here but in heaven. In order to obtain heaven, we must imitate Jesus in all things including the carrying of the Cross.
CHAPTER 4: Make generous use of God's gift of the sacraments in order to strengthen your will. Receive the sacraments of Reconciliation and Holy Eucharist as often as possible.

Carmelite Connections
CHAPTER 3:
1. "With regard to these first Mansions . . . we are tricked by all kinds of deceptions. The devil is less successful with those who are nearer the King's dwelling-place; but at this early stage, as the soul is still absorbed in worldly affairs, engulfed in worldly pleasure and puffed up with worldly honors and ambitions, its vassals, which are the senses and the faculties . . . have not the same power, and such a soul is easily vanquished, although it may desire not to offend God and may perform good works." (*Interior Castle* I.ii.12)
2. "This seems to me to be the condition of a soul which, though not in a bad state, is so completely absorbed in things of the world and so deeply immersed, as I have said, in possessions or honors or business, that, although as a matter of fact it would like

to gaze at the castle and enjoy its beauty, it is prevented from doing so, and seems quite unable to free itself from all these impediments. Everyone, however, who wishes to enter the second Mansions, will be well advised, as far as his state of life permits, to try to put aside all unnecessary affairs and business." (*Interior Castle* I.ii.14)

3. ". .if we are to acquire increasing merit, and not, like Saul and Judas, to be lost, our only possible safety consists in obedience and in never swerving from the law of God; I am referring to those to whom He grants these favors, and in fact to all." (*Interior Castle* V.iii.2)

4. "If you are willing to bear in peace the trial of not being pleased with yourself, you will be offering the Divine Master a home in your heart. It is true that you will suffer, because you will be like a stranger to your own house; but do not be afraid—the poorer you are, the more Jesus will love you. I know that He is better pleased to see you stumbling in the night upon a stony road, than walking in the full light of day upon a path carpeted with flowers, because these flowers might hinder your advance." (*Story of a Soul*, Letter to Celine, V)

5. "She [St. Therese of the Child Jesus] is a very intelligent child, but has not nearly so sweet a disposition as her sister, and her stubbornness is almost unconquerable. When she has said 'No,' nothing will make her change . . ." (*Story of a Soul*, Chapter I)

6. "Oh . . . how little one should think about resting, and how little one should care about honors, and how far one ought to be from wishing to be esteemed in the very least if the Lord makes His special abode in the soul. For if the soul is much with Him, as it is right it should be, it will very seldom think of itself; its whole thought will be concentrated upon finding ways to please Him and upon showing Him how it loves Him. This . . . is the aim of prayer . . ." (*Interior Castle* VII.iv.6)

Although still proceeding through the purgative way and the first mansions, Dilecta is beginning to exhibit some of the characteristics of the Teresian second mansion: a beginning awareness of the conflict between self-will and the divine call, and an increased willingness to embrace sacrifice in order to please Jesus. Matthew's Gospel addresses the matter of doing God's will by quoting Jesus' description of a true disciple, "Not everyone who says to me, 'Lord, Lord,' will enter the kingdom of heaven, but only the one who does the will of my Father in heaven." (7:21) (The purgative way corresponds to the first three Teresian mansions.)

CHAPTER 4:

1. "O Jesus, my Divine Spouse, grant that my baptismal robe may never be sullied. Take me from this world rather than let me stain my soul by committing the least willful fault. May I never seek or find aught but Thee alone!" (*Story of a Soul*, Chapter VIII)

2. "Open, O Jesus, the Book of Life, in which are written the deeds of Thy Saints: all the deeds told in that book I long to have accomplished for Thee." (*Story of a Soul*, Chapter XI)

3. "If we do not give ourselves to His majesty as resolutely as He gives Himself to us, He will be doing more than enough for us if He leaves us in mental prayer and from time to time visits us as He would visit servants in His vineyard. But these others are His

beloved children, whom He would never want to banish from His side; and, as they have no desire to leave Him, He never does so. He seats them at His table, and feeds them with His own food . . ." (*Way of Perfection* XVI.9)

4. "We are like soldiers who, however long they have served, must always be ready for their captain to send them away on any duty which he wants to entrust to them, since it is he who is paying them. And how much better is the payment given by our King than by people on this earth!" (*Way of Perfection* XVIII.3)

5. "As the warriors of old trained their children in the profession of arms, so [Marie] trained me for the battle of life, and roused my ardor by pointing to the victor's glorious palm. She spoke, too, of the imperishable riches which are so easy to amass each day, and of the folly of trampling them under foot when one has but to stoop and gather them. When she talked so eloquently, I was sorry that I was the only one to listen to her teaching, for, in my simplicity, it seemed to me that the greatest sinners would be converted if they but heard her, and that, forsaking the perishable riches of this world, they would seek none but the riches of Heaven." (*Story of a Soul*, Chapter IV)

6. "Each time that my enemy would provoke me to combat, I behave as a gallant soldier. I know that a duel is an act of cowardice, and so, without once looking him in the face, I turn my back on the foe, then I hasten to my Savior . . ." (*Story of a Soul*, Chapter IX)

7. ". . . this person, though by no means perfect, always tried to strengthen her faith, when she communicated, by thinking that it was exactly as if she saw the Lord entering her house, with her own bodily eyes, for she believed in very truth that this Lord was entering her abode, and she ceased, as far as she could, to think of outward things, and went into her abode with Him. She tried to recollect her senses so that they might all become aware of this great blessing, or rather, so that they should not hinder the soul from becoming conscious of it." (*Way of Perfection* XXXIV.8)

8. ". . . it [the soul preparing itself for union with God] begins to utilize the general help which God gives to us all, and to make use of the remedies which He left in His Church—such as frequent confessions, good books, and sermons, for these are the remedies for a soul, dead in negligences and sins and frequently plunged into temptation. The soul begins to live and nourishes itself on this food, and on good meditations, until it is full grown . . ." (*Interior Castle* V.ii.4)

Optional Catechism Lessons

1. First Communicants should complete one of the following:
    a. Continue memorization of catechism questions 46-47 from the flash cards. If possible, visit your parish church to see the confessional. See how many symbols of Christ you can find in the church **or**
    b. Create a banner or poster symbolizing your First Holy Communion; use page 114 of *Jesus Our Life* as a guide or use an original idea.
2. CHAPTER 3: temptation (*Book No. 2* only), and free will (will); CHAPTER 4: the Church and the sacraments

Friday, Week 8 (Day 54)

Parents: Read pages 383-391 in *The Story of a Family.*
High School and Middle School Students: Read the parables outlined on page 87.
First Communicants: Complete "Day 54" in your First Communion journal.
Family Read Aloud: Read Chapters 5 and 6 in *The King of the Golden City.*

Narration
After reading, narrate the events of each chapter.

Parallel Figures Chart
CHAPTER 5: Self, lamp of "Peace"
CHAPTER 6: daily banquet, the white robe, ante-chamber, small stains on the white robe, the jewels with which the King adorned the white robe

Discussion Topics
1. Mother Loyola refers to the "lamp of Peace." What exactly is this lamp to which she refers? Discuss ways to keep your lamp burning. What types of thoughts, words, or actions dim your lamp or cause it to burn out? Do you rely more on Self or your Prince Guardian to help you make decisions? In what ways are you allowing Self to dictate to you? Remember to listen to your Prince Guardian. Ask him to help you remain in the state of grace so that your name continues to be written in the Book of Life.
2. Discuss the advantages and possible pitfalls of receiving Holy Communion as early as the age of seven as well as receiving Him on a daily basis rather than once or twice a month—or only on special feast days. (These regulations regarding the reception of Holy Communion were changed only a few years before this book was written.) Why do you think these laws of the Church were changed?

Searching Scripture
CHAPTER 5: 2 Samuel 22:29, Job 18:5-6; Job 21:17, and Matthew 5:15-16
CHAPTER 6: Song of Songs 2:4, Matthew 22:1-14, and Luke 14:12-14

Growing in Holiness
CHAPTER 5: Develop a plan to help keep not only your lamp but also the lamp of each member of your family burning brightly. What habits or temperaments will need to be eliminated in order to accomplish this? Does your interaction with others need to change in order not to diminish their lamp? Learn from Dilecta's Prince Guardian: Do not try to correct all your faults at once. What can you do to gain strength to persevere in your plan?
CHAPTER 6: Begin to look at Mass as a banquet feast. "Give us today our daily bread"—Matthew 6:11; "Jesus said to them, 'My food is to do the will of the one who sent me and to finish his work'."—John 4:34; and "For my flesh is true food, and my blood is true drink."—John 6:55. Recall that several saints have lived exclusively on the Holy Eucharist. Allow the Bread of Life to fill your spiritual hunger. Try to receive this Food daily.

Carmelite Connections

CHAPTER 5:

1. In discussing the importance of self-knowledge in the first mansions, St. Teresa of Avila states, ". . . self-knowledge is so important that, even if you were raised right up to the heavens, I should like you never to relax your cultivation of it; so long as we are on this earth, nothing matters more to us than humility. And so I repeat that it is a very good thing—excellent, indeed—to begin by entering the room where humility is acquired rather than by flying off to the other rooms. For that is the way to make progress, and, if we have a safe, level road to walk along, why should we desire wings to fly? Let us rather try to get the greatest possible profit out of walking. As I see it, we shall never succeed in knowing ourselves unless we seek to know God . . ." (*Interior Castle* I.ii.9)

2. In regards to traits of the second mansion, St. Teresa says, "The will shows the soul how this true Lover never leaves it, but goes with it everywhere and gives it life and being. Then the understanding comes forward and makes the soul realize that, for however many years it may live, it can never hope to have a better friend, for the world is full of falsehood and these pleasures which the devil pictures to it are accompanied by trials and cares and annoyances; and tells it to be certain that outside this castle it will find neither security nor peace: let it refrain from visiting one house after another when its own house is full of good things, if it will only enjoy them. How fortunate it is to be able to find all that it needs, as it were, at home, especially when it has a Host Who will put all good things into its possession, unless, like the Prodigal Son, it desires to go astray and eat the food of the swine!" (*Interior Castle* II.i.5)

3. "All that the beginner in prayer has to do—and you must not forget this, for it is very important—is to labor and be resolute and prepare himself with all possible diligence to bring his will into conformity with the will of God. . . . you may be quite sure that this comprises the very greatest perfection which can be attained on the spiritual road. The more perfectly a person practices it, the more he will receive of the Lord and the greater the progress he will make on this road." (*Interior Castle* II.i.9)

4. "There is no other remedy for this evil [giving up prayer] . . . except to start again at the beginning; otherwise the soul will keep on losing a little more every day—please God that it may come to realize this." (*Interior Castle* II.i.11)

5. "May it please His Majesty to grant us to understand how much we cost Him, that the servant is not greater than his Lord, that we must . . . work if we would enjoy His glory, and for that reason we must perforce pray, lest we enter continually into temptation." (*Interior Castle* II.i.12)

6. ". . . my soul was yet far from mature, and I had to pass through many trials before reaching the haven of peace, before tasting the delicious fruits of perfect love and of complete abandonment to God's Will." (*Story of a Soul*, Chapter III)

7. ". . . her lamp, filled to the brim with the oil of virtue, burned brightly to the end." (*Story of a Soul*, Epilogue)

Dilecta begins to show more traits of the Teresian second mansions in that she is beginning to learn virtue, she continues to conform her will to the will of God, and she is starting to cheerfully begin again after falling.

CHAPTER 6:

1. "For unless we want to be foolish and to close our minds to facts, we cannot suppose that this is the work of the imagination, as it is when we think of the Lord on the Cross, or of other incidents of the Passion, and picture within ourselves how these things happened. This [receiving Jesus in the Most Holy Sacrament] is something which is happening now; it is absolutely true; and we have no need to go and seek Him somewhere a long way off." (*Way of Perfection* XXXIV.9)

2. "Beneath those accidents of bread, we can approach Him; for, if the King disguises Himself, it would seem that we need not mind coming to Him without so much circumspection and ceremony: by disguising Himself, He has, as it were, obliged Himself to submit to this. Who, otherwise, would dare approach Him so unworthily, with so many imperfections and with such lukewarm zeal?" (*Way of Perfection* XXXIV.10)

3. "Oh, we know not what we ask! How much better does his Wisdom know what we need! He reveals Himself to those who He knows will profit by His presence; though unseen by bodily eyes, He has many ways of revealing Himself to the soul through deep inward emotions and by various other means. Delight to remain with Him; do not lose such an excellent time for talking with Him as the hour after Communion. *Remember that this is a very profitable hour for the soul.*" (*Way of Perfection* XXXIV.11)

4. ". . . we need no wings to go in search of Him but have only to find a place where we can be alone and look upon Him present within us. Nor need we feel strange in the presence of so kind a Guest; we must talk to Him very humbly, as we should to our father, ask Him for things as we should ask a father, tell Him our troubles, beg Him to put them right, and yet realize that we are not worthy to be called His children." (*Way of Perfection* XXVIII.2)

5. "But if we pay no heed to Him save when we have received Him, and go away from Him in search of other and baser things, what can He do? Will He have to drag us by force to look at Him *and be with Him* because He desires to reveal Himself to us? No; for when He revealed himself to all men plainly, and told them clearly who He was, they did not treat Him at all well—very few of them, indeed, even believed Him. So He grants us an exceedingly great favor when He is pleased to show us that it is He Who is in the Most Holy Sacrament. But He will not reveal Himself openly and communicate His glories and bestow His treasure save on those who He knows greatly desire Him, for these are His true friends." (*Way of Perfection* XXXIV.14)

Optional Catechism Lessons

1. First Communicants should complete one of the following:
    a. Complete the memorization of catechism questions 46-47; review all catechism flash cards **or**

    b. Review Lessons 25-28 in *Jesus Our Life* by reviewing questions 34-37, the "Words to Know" from each lesson, the parts of the Mass, the articles used at Mass, and the recommended prayers found on page 117.

2. CHAPTER 5: Actual sin, punishment of Adam (Lesson 5), anger, and theological virtues (virtue); CHAPTER 6: Holy Communion, sacrilege, and confession

Saturday, Week 8 and Week 9, Sunday (Days 55 and 56)

Parents: Finish any reading necessary so that you are prepared to begin on page 391 in *The Story of a Family* on Monday.

High School and Middle School Students: Read the parables outlined on pages 87-88.

First Communicants: Complete an entry in your journal each day this weekend.

Family: Choose an activity in the "Weekend Projects" section of this guide.

Monday, Week 9 (Day 57)

Parents: Read pages 391-398 in *The Story of a Family.*

High School and Middle School Students: Read the parables outlined on page 88.

First Communicants: Complete "Day 57" in your First Communion journal.

Family Read Aloud: Read Chapters 7 and 8 in *The King of the Golden City.*

Narration

After reading, narrate the events of each chapter.

Parallel Figures Chart

Chapter 7: Bridget

Chapter 8: soldiers of the Royal Army, enrolled in my Army, Jolly Ones or Triflers

Discussion Topics

1. Discuss the importance of controlling your free will. How can a well-trained conscience help us in this life's journey?
2. Describe how we are to fight for Christ. What weapons are we to use? Are we expected to fight in open warfare each day? What weapons are to be used each day in fulfilling our daily duty? What more than anything else brings us to victory and reward?

Searching Scripture

CHAPTER 7: Matthew 7:12 and the famous words of Job in Job 1:21-22 ("Job's comforter" refers to one of the three friends of Job who, in consoling him, tried to get him to acknowledge sin, do penance, and submit to God as they believed his suffering was due to sin.)

CHAPTER 8: Matthew 6:19-21, Luke 6:43-45, and Ephesians 6:11-17

Growing in Holiness

CHAPTER 7: Choose a virtue such as patience, perseverance, charity, etc. and practice it every day by saying "no" to your inclination to sin. Ask each morning for your Prince Guardian's help in conquering your Self. Resolve at various times throughout the day to renew this vow through prayer. Each night examine your conscience regarding your thoughts, words, actions, and omissions of that day relative to that virtue. Thank God for His help in your progress, and acknowledge your failures with an act of contrition. Work on this one virtue for at least two weeks before choosing another.

CHAPTER 8: Meditate, if only for a few minutes, each morning before the crucifix. Reminding ourselves frequently of the great sacrifice of love that Jesus made for us can help to keep our priorities correctly ordered. Try to think how long eternity is compared to our span of life on this earth. Keep focused on the importance of pleasing the One who created us, so we may spend all of eternity in His Presence.

Carmelite Connections

CHAPTER 7:

1. "Why, then, do we shrink from interior mortification, since this is the means by which every other kind of mortification may become much more meritorious and perfect,

so that it can then be practiced with greater tranquility and ease? This, as I have said, is acquired by gradual progress and by never indulging our own will and desire, even in small things, until we have succeeded in subduing the body to the spirit." (*Way of Perfection* XII.1)

2. "It is absurd to think that we can enter Heaven without first entering our own souls—without getting to know ourselves, and reflecting on the wretchedness of our nature and what we owe to God, and continually imploring His mercy . . . if we never look at Him or think of what we owe Him, and of the death which He suffered for our sakes, I do not see how we can get to know Him or do good works in His service. For what can be the value of faith without works, or of works which are not united with the merits of our Lord Jesus Christ? And what but such thoughts can arouse us love this Lord?" (*Interior Castle* II.i.12)

CHAPTER 8:

1. "What a strange thing! You might suppose that the devil never tempted those who do not walk along the road of prayer!" (*Way of Perfection* XXXIX.7)

2. ". . . wherever the king is, or so they say, the court is too; that is to say, wherever God is, there is Heaven. No doubt, you can believe that in any place where His Majesty is, there is fullness of glory. Remember how St. Augustine tells us about his seeking God in many places and eventually finding Him within himself." (*Way of Perfection* XXVIII.2)

Optional Catechism Lessons

1. First Communicants should complete one of the following:
   a. In *The New Saint Joseph First Communion Catechism*, read Lesson 11 **or**
   b. In *Jesus Our Life* from the Faith and Life series, read Lesson 29; review question 38, and the "Words to Know." How can you be an apostle?

2. CHAPTER 7: Two Great Commandments (Lesson 15), conscience, hope, and virtue; CHAPTER 8: faith, prayer, Confirmation, and the indelible mark of Confirmation (Lesson 23)

Tuesday, Week 9 (Day 58)

Parents: Read pages 399-409 in *The Story of a Family*.

High School and Middle School Students: Read the parables outlined on page 88.

First Communicants: Complete "Day 58" in your First Communion journal.

Family Read Aloud: Read Chapters 9 and 10 in *The King of the Golden City*.

Narration

After reading, narrate the events of each chapter.

Parallel Figures Chart

CHAPTER 9: wounded soldiers, sullied white robe

CHAPTER 10: master of his own house, soft knock at the door

Discussion Topics

1. God provides for all our needs. But we may not always make use of the opportunities for increased grace that He offers us. Discuss the main reasons many commit sin. How can you apply this knowledge to increase your chances of victory in the fight?

2. Why is it important to pay the debt our sins have incurred for us? What happens if we die with this debt unpaid? What does Jesus do to give us the opportunity to pay off this debt?

Searching Scripture

CHAPTER 9: Matthew 7: 7-11 and Luke 11:3

CHAPTER 10: Sirach 33:28, Matthew 5:23-26, and Colossians 2:13-14

Growing in Holiness

CHAPTER 9: Ask each day for the graces that you need to fight your sinful habits and to avoid occasions of sin. If you are not able to receive Communion daily, make a spiritual communion often during the day—especially in times of temptation or tiredness.

CHAPTER 10: Think of at least three practical things you can do to start making reparation for your sins and the sins of the whole world right now. Ask your guardian angel each day to help you not only to watch for opportunities to make reparation but also to make the best possible use of them.

Carmelite Connections

CHAPTER 9:

1. "Show us then, O our good Master, some way in which we may live through this most dangerous warfare without frequent surprise. The best way we can do this . . . is to use the love and fear given us by His Majesty. For love will make us quicken our steps, while fear will make us look where we are setting our feet so that we shall not fall on the road where there are so many obstacles. Along that road all living creatures must pass, and if we have these two things we shall certainly not be deceived." (*Way of Perfection* XL.1)

2. "Keep this in mind, for it is very important advice, so do not neglect it until you find you have such a fixed determination not to offend the Lord that you would rather lose a thousand lives, *and be persecuted by the whole world*, than commit one mortal sin, and until you are most careful not to commit venial sins. I am referring now to sins committed knowingly: as far as those of the other kind are concerned, who can fail to commit these frequently? . . . From any sin, however small, committed with full knowledge, may God deliver us, especially since we are sinning against so great a Sovereign and realizing that He is watching us! . . . If we commit a sin in this way, however slight, it seems to me that our offence is not small but very, very great." (*Way of Perfection* XLI.5)

3. "He prays for nothing more than this 'to-day' since He has given us this most holy Bread. He has given it to us forever . . . as the sustenance and manna of humanity. We can have it whenever we please and we shall not die of hunger save through our own

fault . . . *He teaches us to fix our desires upon heavenly things and to pray that we may begin to enjoy these things while here on earth. . . ."* (*Way of Perfection* XXXIV.2)

4. "I have often observed that Our Lord will not give me any store of provisions, but nourishes me each moment with food that is ever new; I find it within me without knowing how it has come there. I simply believe that it is Jesus Himself hidden in my poor heart, who is secretly at work, inspiring me with what He wishes me to do as each occasion arises." (*Story of a Soul*, Chapter VIII)

5. ". . . the Lord says: 'Ask, and it shall be given you.' If you do not believe His Majesty in those passages of His Gospel where He gives us this assurance, it will be of little help to you . . . for me to weary my brains by telling you of it. Still, I will say to anyone who is in doubt that she will lose little by putting the matter to the test; for this journey has the advantage of giving us *very much* more than we ask or shall even get so far as to desire. This is a never-failing truth; I know it." (*Way of Perfection* XXIII.6)

The beginning stage of those striving for perfection—the purgative way—in which the struggle against temptation and sin is paramount is characterized in this chapter. Dilecta continues her journey toward the Golden City still within this first classical stage of perfection. Within the mansions of St. Teresa, Dilecta remains in the second mansion, typified by her desire to conform her will to God's will and her interest in using the tools God has provided to ward off temptation and remain in the state of grace.

CHAPTER 10:

1. ". . . all of his [the devil's] powers are in the external sphere." (*Interior Castle* VI.ii.6)

2. "Remember that in few of the mansions of this castle are we free from struggles with devils. . . . in some of them, the wardens, who . . . are the faculties, have the strength for the fight; but . . . we should not cease to be watchful against the devil's wiles, lest he deceive us in the guise of an angel of light. For there are a multitude of ways in which he can deceive us, and gradually make his way into the castle, and until he is actually there we do not realize it." (*Interior Castle* I.ii.15)

3. "May His Majesty be pleased to grant us *to experience* this before He takes us from this life, for it will be a great thing at the hour of death, *when we are going we know not whither*, to realize that we shall be judged by One Whom we have loved above all things. . . . Once our debts have been paid we shall be able to walk in safety. We shall not be going into a foreign land, but into our own country, for it belongs to Him Whom we have loved so truly and Who Himself loves us. Remember . . . the greatness of the gain which comes from this love, and of our loss if we do not possess it, for in that case we shall be delivered into the hands of the tempter . . ." (*Way of Perfection* XL.8)

4. "What a wonderful thing it is. . .to have a wise and prudent Master who foresees our perils. . . . No words could ever exaggerate the importance of this. The Lord, then, saw it was necessary to awaken such souls and to remind them that they have enemies, and how much greater danger they are in if they are unprepared . . ." (*Way of Perfection* XXXVII.7)

Optional Catechism Lessons
1. First Communicants should complete one of the following:
   a. Answer the questions at the end of Lesson 11 in the First Communion Ca-techism; begin memorization of catechism questions 48-54 **or**
   b. Read Lesson 30 in *Jesus Our Life* from the Faith and Life series; review ques-tion 39 and the "Words to Know." Memorize the seven sacraments.
2. CHAPTER 9: mortal sin, venial sin, and how to keep from committing sin (Lesson 6 in *Book No. 2* only); CHAPTER 10: remission of sin (*Book No. 2* only), reparation (*Book No. 2* only), merit (*Book No. 2* only), temporal punishment and indulgence

Wednesday, Week 9 (Day 59)

Parents: Read pages 409-419 in *The Story of a Family*.
High School and Middle School Students: Read the parables outlined on page 88.
First Communicants: Complete "Day 59" in your First Communion journal.
Family Read Aloud: Read Chapter 11 in *The King of the Golden City*.

Narration
After reading, narrate the events of this chapter.

Parallel Figures Chart
the fair, the play, Daisy, the broad road

Discussion Topics
Daisy may be defined as one of the Jolly Ones—a Trifler. Oftentimes the pressure Christians receive from Triflers is hard to resist. Discuss the technique Dilecta uses. What else might she have done to resist Daisy and the other girls? What can you do when you are pressured by others to participate in a sinful action?

Searching Scripture
Psalm 95:7-9, Proverbs 1:8-15, Proverbs 4:10-27, Sirach 21:1-6, and Matthew 7:13-14

Growing in Holiness
Dilecta gives in to her Prince Guardian when she feels his prayers for her. Recite often the prayer to your guardian angel asking for his guidance and spiritual help. Remember the power of prayer. Pray often the Our Father—"Lead us not into temptation but de-liver us from evil" and the Hail Mary—"Pray for us sinners now and at the hour of our death." Pray not only for yourself but also for others.

Carmelite Connections
1. "How often people stray through not taking advice, especially when there is a risk of doing someone harm!" (*Way of Perfection* IV.14)
2. "You already know that the first stone of this foundation must be a good conscience and that you must make every effort to free yourselves from even venial sins and fol-low the greatest possible perfection." (*Way of Perfection* V.3)

3. "A . . . reason why we must be resolute is that this will give the devil less opportunity to tempt us. He is very much afraid of resolute souls, knowing by experience that they inflict great injury upon him, and, when he plans to do them harm he only profits them and others and is himself the loser. We must not become unwatchful, or count upon this, for we have to do with treacherous folk, who are great cowards and dare not attack the wary, but, if they see we are careless, will work us great harm. And if they know anyone to be changeable, and not resolute in *doing* what is good and firmly determined to persevere, they will not leave him alone either by night or by day and will suggest to him endless misgivings and difficulties." (*Way of Perfection* XXIII.4)

4. ". . . if they lose their Guide, the good Jesus, they will be unable to find their way. . ." (*Interior Castle* VI.vii.7)

5. ". . . as if we could arrive at these Mansions by letting others make the journey for us! That is not possible . . . so, for the love of the Lord, let us make a real effort; let us leave our reason and fears in His hands and let us forget the weakness of our nature which is apt to cause us so much worry." (*Interior Castle* III.ii.9)

6. "Do not be dismayed . . . at the number of things which you have to consider before setting out on this Divine journey, which is the royal road to Heaven. By taking this road, we gain such precious treasures that it is no wonder if the cost seems to us a high one. The time will come when we shall realize that all we have paid has been nothing at all by comparison with the greatness of our prize. Let us now return to those who wish to travel on this road. . . . It is most important—all important, indeed—that they should begin well by making an earnest and most determined resolve not to halt until they reach their goal . . . however hard they may have to labor . . ." (*Way of Perfection* XXI.1-2)

7. "For it is as if He [Christ] had said: In truth the way is very strait, more so than you think. . . . He says first that the gate is strait, to make it clear that, in order for the soul to enter by this gate, which is Christ, and which comes at the beginning of the road, the will must first be straitened and detached in all things sensual and temporal, and God must be loved above them all. . . . For this path ascending the high mountain of perfection leads upward, and is narrow, and therefore requires travelers that have no burden weighing upon them with respect to lower things, neither aught that embarrasses them with respect to higher things: God alone must be the object of our search and attainment." (*Ascent to Mount Carmel* II.VII.7)

8. "What a strange idea that one could ever expect to travel on a road infested by thieves, for the purpose of gaining some great treasure, without running into danger! Worldly people like to take life peaceably; but they will deny themselves sleep, *perhaps* for nights on end, in order to gain a farthing's profit, and they will leave you no peace either of body or of soul. If, when you are on the way to gaining this treasure . . . and are traveling by this royal road—this safe road trodden by our King and by His elect and His saints—if even then they tell you it is full of danger and make you

so afraid, what will be the dangers encountered by those who think they will be able to gain this treasure and yet are not on the road to it?" (*Way of Perfection* XXI.5)

9. ". . . never pay heed to . . . matters of popular opinion. This is no time for believing everyone; believe only those whom you see modeling their lives on the life of Christ. Endeavour always to have a good conscience; practice humility; despise all worldly things; and believe firmly in the teaching of our Holy Mother Church. You may then be quite sure that you are on a [very] good road." (*Way of Perfection* XXI.10)

Dilecta continues through the second mansions by beginning to learn virtue, continuing the battle against her will, and by being concerned about good companionship.

Optional Catechism Lessons
1. First Communicants should complete one of the following:
   a. Write catechism questions 48-54 from *The New Saint Joseph First Communion Catechism* on index cards and review **or**
   b. Read Lesson 31 in *Jesus Our Life* from the Faith and Life series; review questions 40-42 and the "Words to Know." If you have not yet memorized the Apostles' Creed, do so now. Who is pictured on page 126?
2. Fourth Commandment (Lesson 19), Sixth Commandment (Lesson 19), saint, and temptation (*Book No. 2* only)

Thursday, Week 9 (Day 60)
Parents: Read pages 420-427 in *The Story of a Family*.
High School and Middle School Students: Read the parables outlined on page 88.
First Communicants: Complete "Day 60" in your First Communion journal.
Family Read Aloud: Read Chapter 12 in *The King of the Golden City*.

Narration
After reading, narrate the events of this chapter.

Parallel Figures Chart
bad sweets sprinkled with sugar, poisonous powders, Dark Valley

Discussion Topics
What are some signs that the devil is near? How can we frighten him away?

Searching Scripture
Luke 4:36, Romans 16:19-20, 2 Corinthians 2:11, and Philippians 2:5-11

Growing in Holiness
When tempted by the devil or aware of his influence and presence, rebuke him in the name of Jesus. Remember how cowardly he is when the name of Jesus is spoken. Memorize Psalm 124:8. Be sure to make the sign of the cross whenever you hear the name of Jesus used as a curse or in blasphemy. Unfortunately, this sin is viewed as acceptable behavior by many in our society and is widely used in the media.

Carmelite Connections

1. "Happily for me, I had visible guardian angels to guide me. . . . they chose books suitable to my age, which interested me and at the same time provided food for my thoughts and affections." (*Story of a Soul*, Chapter IV)

2. "But the devil comes with his artful wiles, and, under the color of doing good, sets about undermining it in trivial ways, and involving it in practices which, so he gives it to understand, are not wrong; little by little he darkens its understanding, and weakens its will, and causes its self-love to increase, until in one way and another he begins to withdraw it from the love of God and to persuade it to indulge its own wishes." (*Interior Castle*, V.iv.7)

3. "Beware also . . . of certain kinds of humility which the devil inculcates in us and which make us very uneasy about the gravity of our *past sins*. There are many ways in which he is accustomed to depress us so that in time we withdraw from Communion and give up our private prayer . . . [a soul] loses confidence and sits with her hands in her lap because she thinks she can do nothing well . . ." (*Way of Perfection* XXXIX.1)

4. "'Peace, peace,' said the Lord . . . unless we have peace, and strive for peace in our own home, we shall not find it in the homes of others. Let this war now cease. By the blood which Christ shed for us, I beg this of those who have not begun to enter within themselves; and those who have begun to do so must not allow such warfare to turn them back. . .let them place their trust, not in their themselves, but in the mercy of God, and they will see how His Majesty can lead them on from one groups of Mansions to another and set them on safe ground . . ." (*Interior Castle* II.i.10)

Optional Catechism Lessons

1. First Communicants should complete one of the following:
   a. Have someone read to you the story of the Last Supper in the Bible in Matthew 26: 26-30. Leonardo da Vinci created a very famous painting of this scene. Draw or paint a picture of the Last Supper or of the priest during the consecration. Continue memorization of catechism questions 1-54 from the flash cards **or**
   b. Read Lesson 32 in *Jesus Our Life*; review the "Words to Know." Become familiar with the mysteries of the rosary and how to pray the rosary.

2. scruples (Use a Catholic dictionary.), Second Commandment (Lesson 18), happiness, and temperance (*Book No. 2* only)

Friday, Week 9 (Day 61)

Parents: Read pages 427-436 in *The Story of a Family*.
High School and Middle School Students: Read the parables outlined on page 88.
First Communicants: Complete "Day 61" in your First Communion journal.
Family Read Aloud: Read Chapters 13 and 14 in *The King of the Golden City*.

Narration

After reading, narrate the events of each chapter.

Parallel Figures Chart
CHAPTER 14: foot slipped in crossing the road, car came and drove over you
CHAPTER 15: brave little soldier

Discussion Topics
1. If you commit a venial sin, what is the best thing to do? How can you prevent a venial sin—or a small bad habit—from becoming a mortal sin? Why is it important to make a good act of contrition after committing any sin?
2. What were some of the traits that the King loved in Dilecta? (The word "Dilecta" means "beloved.") What do you think are some of the things He loves about you? Why was Jesus pleased with Dilecta even though she gave in to her anger? Why is it important to keep trying even when we sin?

Searching Scripture
CHAPTER 13: Sirach 30:8, Luke 16:10, John 12:24-26, and Galatians 5:16-26
CHAPTER 14: Psalm 37:1-11, Mark 8:34-38, Luke 12:6-9, I Corinthians 9:24-26, and Colossians 3:23

Growing in Holiness
CHAPTER 13: Try to please Jesus in all you do. When you find yourself being selfish, disobedient, or sulky, make a good act of contrition and begin anew immediately. Jesus forgives us as soon as we ask. He never tires of forgiving us, as His love for us is perfect.
CHAPTER 14: As you make your examination of conscience each night, be sure to include all the times you fought off sin. Try to avoid the occasions or conditions that cause you to sin. Thank Jesus as well as your guardian angel for helping you to persevere in the battle against sin. Trust in God and His mercy. Never give up the fight against sin!

Carmelite Connections
CHAPTER 13:
1. "... we shall learn to subdue our wills in everything; for if ... you are very careful *about your prayer*, you will *soon* find yourselves gradually reaching the summit of the mountain without knowing how. But how harsh it sounds to say that we must take pleasure in nothing, unless we also say what consolations and delights this renunciation brings in its train, and what a great gain it is, even in this life!" (*Way of Perfection* XII.3)
2. "But it is one thing to commit a sin knowingly and after long deliberation, and quite another to do it so suddenly that the knowledge of its being a venial sin and its commission are one and the same thing, and we hardly realize what we have done ... *remember the importance of habit and of starting to realize what a serious thing it is to offend Him* ... for our life, and much more than our life, depends upon this virtue [fear of the Lord] being firmly planted in our souls. Until you are conscious within your soul of possessing it, you need always to exercise very great care and to avoid all occasions of sin and any kind of company which will not help you to get nearer to God. Be most careful, in all that you do, to bend your will to it; see that all you say tends to edification; flee from all places where there is conversation which is not thoroughly

impressed upon the soul; though, if one has true love, it is quickly acquired." (*Way of Perfection* XLI.5-6)

3. ". . . an obedience so *extremely* strict that we never go an inch beyond the superior's orders, knowing that these orders come from God. . . . It is to this duty of obedience that you must attach the greatest importance." (*Way of Perfection* XVIII.7)

4. ". . . when the way of perfection was opened out before me, I realized that in order to become a Saint one must suffer much, always seek the most perfect path, and forget oneself. I also understood that there are many degrees of holiness, that each soul is free to respond to the calls of Our Lord, to do much or little for His Love—in a word, to choose amongst the sacrifices He asks." (*Story of a Soul*, Chapter I)

CHAPTER 14:

1. "[God] will also manifest very clearly that he alone is truth and cannot lie. . .if we are in any way to grow like our God. . .we shall do well always to study earnestly to walk in this truth. I do not mean simply that we must not tell falsehoods. . . . I mean that we should walk in truth, in the presence of God and man, in every way possible to us. In particular we must not desire to be reputed better than we are and in all we do we must attribute to God what is His and to ourselves what is ours, and try to seek after truth in everything. If we do that, we shall make small account of this world, for it is all lying and falsehood and for that reason cannot endure." (*Interior Castle* VI.x.5-6)

2. ". . . this King, Who, unskilled though I am in speaking with Him, does not refuse to hear me or forbid me to approach Him, or command His guards to throw me out. For the angels in His presence know well that their King is such that He prefers the unskilled language of a humble peasant boy, knowing that he would say more if he had more to say, to the speech of the wisest and most learned men, however elegant may be their arguments, if these are not accompanied by humility. But we must not be unmannerly because He is good. . . . When you approach God, then, try to think and realize Whom you are about to address and continue to do so while you are addressing Him. If we had a thousand lives, we should never fully understand how this Lord merits that we behave toward Him, before Whom even the angels tremble. He orders all things and He can do all things; with Him to will is to perform. . . . do not, I beg you, address God while you are thinking of other things . . ." (*Way of Perfection* XXII.4, 7-8)

3. "Another reason [for beginning with determination] . . . is that a resolute person fights more courageously. He knows that, come what may, he must not retreat. He is like a soldier in battle who is aware that if he is vanquished, his life will not be spared and that if he escapes death in battle he must die afterwards. *It has been proved, I think, that* such a man will fight more resolutely and will try, as they say, to sell his life dearly, fearing the enemy's blows the less because he understands the importance of victory and know that his very life depends upon his gaining it." (*Way of Perfection* XXIII.5)

4. "It will profit me little if I am alone and deeply recollected, and make acts of love to Our Lord and plan and promise to work wonders in His service, and then, as soon as I leave my retreat and some occasion presents itself, I do just the opposite. . . . For,

when He sees a very timorous soul, He sends it . . . some very sore trial . . . and later, when the soul becomes aware of this, it loses its fear and offers itself to Him the more readily." (*Interior Castle* VII.iv.7)

Optional Catechism Lessons

1. First Communicants should complete one of the following:
    a. Complete memorization of catechism questions 48-54 from Lesson 11 in *The New Saint Joseph First Communion Catechism* **or**
    b. Review Lessons 1-32 in *Jesus Our Life* by reviewing questions 1-42 as well as the "Words to Know" from each lesson. The memorization of the prayers contained at the back of the book should be nearly complete.
2. CHAPTER 13: Vicar of Christ (*Book No. 2* only), forgive, and contrition (perfect and imperfect); CHAPTER 14: Eighth Commandment (Lesson 20), truth, despair, and Perfections of God—especially all-present and all-knowing (Lesson 2)

Saturday, Week 9 and Week 10, Sunday (Days 62 and 63)

Parents: Finish any reading necessary so that you are prepared to begin on page 436 in *The Story of a Family* on Monday.

High School and Middle School Students: Read the parables outlined on page 88.

First Communicants: Complete an entry in your journal each day this weekend.

Family: Choose an activity in the "Weekend Projects" section of this guide.

Monday, Week 10 (Day 64)

Parents: Read pages 436-442 in *The Story of a Family*.
High School and Middle School Students: Read the parables outlined on page 88.
First Communicants: Complete "Day 64" in your First Communion journal.
Family Read Aloud: Read Chapter 15 in *The King of the Golden City*.

Narration

After reading, narrate the events of this chapter.

Parallel Figures Chart

princesses

Discussion Topics

1. The King compares His love to the sunshine. What other comparisons can you make for His love?
2. Read St. Paul's treatise on love in 1 Corinthians 13:4-7. Choose one characteristic of love from this passage, and write or discuss how you might live out that love within your daily family life.

Searching Scripture

Luke 6:27-35, Luke 10:3, John 13:34-35, Romans 12:1-2, and Ephesians 5:10.

Growing in Holiness

If possible, go to a church or chapel and pray the Stations of the Cross. Or use a meditation book to perform this devotion at home. Try each day to share with Jesus the day's events and your struggles in serving Him. Remember that He wants to hear not only about your successes in conquering sin but also your failures—not only of your love for Him but also of all the tiny details of your day. Make little presents to Him throughout the day by offering Him your sacrifices, your trials, and your thanksgivings.

Carmelite Connections

1. "As the sun shines both on the cedar and on the floweret, so the Divine Sun illumines every soul, great and small . . ." (*Story of a Soul*, Chapter 1)
2. ". . . the Father of lights . . . Who, like the sun's ray, sheds His blessings abundantly without respect of persons, whenever there is cause, showing Himself likewise joyfully to men as they walk in the roads and paths . . . all over the round earth." (*Living Flame* 1.15)
3. ". . . You must not despise this first favor . . . even though you have not responded immediately to the Lord's call; for His Majesty is quite prepared to wait many days and even years, especially when He sees we are persevering and have good desires. This is the most necessary thing . . . [in the second mansions]; if we have this, we can not fail to gain greatly. Nevertheless, the assault which the devils now make upon the soul, in all kinds of ways, is terrible; and the soul suffers more than in the preceding Mansions . . ." (*Interior Castle* II.i.4)

Dilecta is entering the illuminative stage and the third Teresian mansions. Jesus is increasingly becoming the center of her life. She tries to imitate Him and is growing in the theological virtues. Characteristic of the third mansions, she is careful not to offend God, avoiding even venial sins. Her love for penance is growing, and she is cautious of her speech. Many spend much time in the first three mansions: "It seems that, in order to reach these Mansions [the fourth and beyond], one must have lived for a long time in the others." (*Interior Castle* V.i.1) (Note that the illuminative way roughly corresponds to the fourth through sixth Teresian mansions.)

Optional Catechism Lessons
1. First Communicants should complete one of the following:
   a. In the First Communion Catechism, read the section on "The Holy Mass" and feasts and Holy Days of Obligation on pages 53-61 **or**
   b. In *Jesus Our Life*, read Lesson 33. Sometime this week go to your parish church and pray the Divine Praises before Jesus in the tabernacle.
2. Stations of the Cross and envy

Tuesday, Week 10 (Day 65)
Parents: Read pages 443-453 in *The Story of a Family*.
High School and Middle School Students: Read the parables outlined on page 88.
First Communicants: Complete "Day 65" in your First Communion journal.
Family Read Aloud: Read Chapter 16 in *The King of the Golden City*.

Narration
After reading, narrate the events of this chapter.

Parallel Figures Chart
own country, Palace, a work to do, lens

Discussion Topics
1. St. Augustine stated, "You have made us for Yourself, and our heart is restless until it rests in You." Explain this statement in light of the content of this chapter.
2. What does Jesus tell Dilecta about the gift of faith? What does this gift enable her to do? How can the light of faith be kept bright?

Searching Scripture
Psalm 118:24, Matthew 6:19-21, Matthew 7:21-27, Matthew 19:23-24, Matthew 24:36-44, Matthew 25:21, Luke 12:15, Hebrews 13:14, Ephesians 2:19-22, 1 Corinthians 13:12, 2 Corinthians 3:18, Revelation 12:1, and Revelation 21:1-27

Growing in Holiness
In this chapter, Jesus complains to Dilecta that many people neglect the task of perfecting themselves. Instead, many people spend their time and energy gathering material goods and doing nothing but enjoy themselves. In Scripture too Jesus cautions us against storing up treasures that are not heavenly treasures. Do a thorough inventory of your priorities—not what you say your priorities are but what your actions show them to be. If

you are not busy preparing yourself for your heavenly home but rather are making yourself very comfortable here on earth, maybe you need to make some changes. Make sure your salvation and the salvation of others is your first priority.

Carmelite Connections

1. ". . . imagine that we have within us a palace of priceless worth, built entirely of gold and precious stones—a palace. . . fit for so great a Lord. Imagine that it is partly your doing that this palace should be what it is—and this is really true, for there is no building so beautiful as a soul that is pure and full of virtues, and, the greater the virtues are, the more brilliantly do the stones shine. Imagine that within the palace dwells this great King . . . Who is seated upon a throne of supreme price—namely, your heart." (*Way of Perfection* XXVIII.10)

2. ". . . the Lord knows everyone as he really is and gives each his work to do—according to what He sees to be most fitting for his soul, and for His own Self, and for the good of his neighbor. . . . It is well that the Lord should see that we are not leaving anything undone." (*Way of Perfection* XVIII.3)

3. ". . . death has come to many people I knew then, young, rich, and happy. I recall to mind the delightful places where they lived, and ask myself where they are now, and what profit they derive today from the beautiful houses and grounds where I saw them enjoying all the good things of this life, and I reflect that 'All is vanity besides loving God and serving Him alone.'" (*Story of a Soul*, Chapter IV)

4. "Oh, what a mockery is everything in the world if it does not lead us and help us towards this end—and would be even though all the worldly delights and riches and joys that we can imagine were to last forever! For everything is cloying and degrading by comparison with these treasures, which we shall enjoy eternally. And even these are nothing by comparison with having for our own the Lord of all treasures and of Heaven and earth." (*Interior Castle* VI.iv.10)

5. "You are really the daughters of Our Lady. . . . Imitate Our Lady and consider how great she must be . . ." (*Interior Castle* III.i.3)

6. "He [the King] reveals Himself to those who He knows will profit by His presence; unseen by bodily eyes, He has many ways of revealing Himself to the soul through deep inward emotions and by various other means." (*Way of Perfection* XXXIV.11)

7. ". . . reason tells the soul how mistaken it is in thinking that all these earthly things are of the slightest value by comparison with what it is seeking; faith instructs it in what it must do to find satisfaction; memory shows it how all these things come to an end, and reminds it that those who have derived too much enjoyment from the things which it has seen have died. Sometimes they have died suddenly and been quickly forgotten by all." (*Interior Castle* II.i.5)

8. ". . . teaching me where our true home is and . . . showing me that on earth we are but pilgrims; it is a great thing to see what is awaiting us there and to know where we are going to live. For if a person has to go and settle in another country, it is a great help to him in bearing the trials of the journey if he has found out that it is a country where he will be able to live in complete comfort. It also makes it easy for us to die

if we think upon heavenly things and try to have our conversation in Heaven. This is a great advantage for us: merely to look up towards the heavens makes the soul re-collected, for, as the Lord has been pleased to reveal some part of what is there, the thought dwells upon it." (*Life of the Holy Mother Teresa of Jesus* XXXVIII.6)

9. ". . . when we are wearied with traveling . . . the Lord grants . . . our soul quiet, and while they are in that state He give us a clear understanding of the nature of the gifts He bestows upon those whom He bring to His Kingdom . . . which will give them a great hope of eventually attaining to a perpetual enjoyment of what on earth He only allows them to taste." (*Way of Perfection* XXX.7)

Optional Catechism Lessons
1. First Communicants should complete one of the following:
    a. Use a missal to become familiar with the parts of the Mass as well as the or-der of the special readings and prayers for each day. If a missal is not available, borrow a missalette from the church. Continue the memorization of the ca-techism questions as well as the prayers **or**
    b. Read Lesson 34 in *Jesus Our Life* from the Faith and Life series; review the "Words to Know."
2. Blessed Virgin Mary (Lesson 5 and *Book No. 2* only, Lesson 12), and faith

Wednesday, Week 10 (Day 66)
Parents: Read pages 454-459 in *The Story of a Family*.
High School and Middle School Students: Read the parables outlined on page 88.
First Communicants: Complete "Day 66" in your First Communion journal.
Family Read Aloud: Read Chapters 17 and 18 in *The King of the Golden City*.

Narration
After reading, narrate the events of each chapter.

Parallel Figures Chart
CHAPTER 17: Land of Weary Waiting
CHAPTER 18: save up her pennies

Discussion Topics
1. What were the three directions in which Dilecta could turn her lens? How might our thoughts and actions be different if we too could see these things? Describe the pains of Purgatory. How can we avoid them? What can we do to aid the many suffering souls in Purgatory? Why must we prize the gift of faith?
2. How important is it to feel the presence (and presents) of Jesus? Why must we per-severe even when we do not feel like we are making progress in our spiritual life or doing anything at all to please Jesus? What role do both silence and feelings play in our prayer life?

Searching Scripture
CHAPTER 17: 2 Maccabees 12:42-46, Luke 17:5-6, 1 Corinthians 3:13-15, and Revelation 20:12-15
CHAPTER 18: Matthew 10:40-42, Matthew 25:34-46, and at least three of the following psalms: Psalm 27, Psalm 42:1-6, Psalm 62, Psalm 63, Psalm 116, Psalm 131, Psalm 139, or Psalm 150

Growing in Holiness
CHAPTER 17: Offer up your prayers, actions, and sacrifices each day for the holy souls in Purgatory. Remember to pray for them when you pass a cemetery. Add a simple prayer for them after your mealtime prayer or within your morning or evening prayers. Ask your guardian angel (Angel means "messenger.") to deliver these prayers and sacrifices to the suffering souls.
CHAPTER 18: Try to receive Jesus in the Blessed Sacrament every day. Visit Him in the tabernacle as often as possible. Remember to watch for His face, not His hands when He comes to you. Bring gifts to Him rather than waiting for His gifts to you. Try to advance in the spiritual life so that the most important thing for you is not your feelings of happiness and peace, but the satisfaction of knowing that you are pleasing Him even though you do not feel His peace or His presence.

Carmelite Connections
CHAPTER 17:
1. "Then [in heaven] we shall be amazed to see how different His judgment is from the ideas which we have formed on earth." (*Interior Castle* VI.viii.10)
2. "Lord, how Thou doest afflict Thy lovers. . . . It is well that great things should cost a great deal, especially if the soul can be purified by suffering and enabled to enter the seventh Mansion, just as those who are to enter Heaven are cleansed in purgatory." (*Interior Castle* VI.xi.6)
3. "How sweet will be the death of those who have done penance for all their sins and have not to go to purgatory! It may be that they will begin to enjoy glory even in this world, and will know no fear, but only peace." (*Way of Perfection* XL.9)
4. ". . . how much more sensitive the soul is than the body. . . . this suffering resembles that of souls in purgatory; despite their being no longer in the body they suffer much more than do those who are still in the body and on earth." (*Interior Castle* VI.xi.3)
5. ". . . let us consider the condition of those who are in hell. . . . the torment suffered by the soul is much more acute than that suffered by the body. . . . These unhappy souls know that they will have to suffer in this way forever and ever . . ." (*Interior Castle* VI.xi.7)
6. "What does it matter if I am in Purgatory until the Day of Judgment provided a single soul should be saved through my prayer? And how much less does it matter if many souls profit by it and the Lord is honored!" (*Way of Perfection* III.6)

CHAPTER 18:

1. "For often it is God's will that His elect should be conscious of their misery and so He withdraws His help from them a little—and no more than that is needed to make us recognize our limitations very quickly. They then realize that this is a way of testing them, for they gain a clear perception of their shortcomings, and sometimes they derive more pain from finding that, in spite of themselves, they are still grieving about earthly things, and not very important things either, than from the matter which is troubling them. This, I think, is a great mercy on the part of God, and even though they are at fault they gain a great deal in humility." (*Interior Castle* III.ii.2)

2. "Having won such great favors, the soul . . . has the keenest longings for death, and so it frequently and tearfully begs God to take it out of this exile. Everything in this life that it sees wearies it; when it finds itself alone it experiences great relief, but immediately this distress returns till it hardly knows itself when it is without it." (*Interior Castle* VI.vi.1)

3. "[The King] never takes His eyes off you. . . . He has borne with thousands of foul and abominable sins which you have committed against him, yet even they have not been enough to make Him cease looking upon you. Is it such a great matter, then, for you to avert the eyes *of your soul* from outward things and sometimes to look at Him? See, He is only waiting for us to look at Him. He longs so much for us to look at Him once more that it will not be for lack of effort on His part if we fail to do so." (*Way of Perfection* XXVI.3)

4. In referring to souls in the fourth mansions, St. Teresa states, "A person who used to be afraid of doing penance . . . now believes that in God he can to everything, and has more desire to do such things than he had previously. The fear of trials that he was wont to have is now largely assuaged, because he has a more lively faith, and realizes that, if he endures these trials for God's sake, His Majesty will give him grace to bear them patiently, and sometimes even to desire them, because he also cherishes a great desire to do something for God. The better he gets to know the great-ness of God, the better he comes to realize the misery of his own condition; having now tasted the consolations of God, he sees that earthly things are mere refuse; so, little by little, he withdraws from them and in this way becomes more his own master. In short, he finds himself strengthened in all the virtues and will infallibly contin-ue to increase in them unless he turns back and commits offences against God." (*Interior Castle* IV.iii.9)

Dilecta is now in the classical unitive stage of perfection as characterized by the habitual, intimate union with God through Jesus; a delight in prayer; living continually in the presence of God; great mastery over self; constant loving and lingering thoughts of God; all virtues infused with love; and a simplification of her life in that prayer is no longer at set times but permeates her whole life.

Optional Catechism Lessons
1. First Communicants should complete one of the following:
   a. Begin to test the memorization of catechism questions 1-54 as well as the Ten Commandments, the seven sacraments, and the prayers **or**
   b. Spend today and tomorrow reviewing questions 1-42 in *Jesus Our Life*. Review too the "Words to Know" on pages 141-147.
2. CHAPTER 17: Purgatory, temporal punishment, judgment (*Book No. 2* only—particular and general), and Hell; CHAPTER 18: corporal and spiritual works of mercy (*Book No. 2* only) and dark night of the soul (Use a Catholic dictionary.)

Thursday, Week 10 (Day 67)

Parents: If possible, make a holy hour with the entire family in church to ask Jesus to grant a special zeal and appreciation for the Sacrament of Holy Eucharist for your entire family. Read the Passion of our Lord (Luke Chapter 22, Verse 14 through Chapter 23).

High School and Middle School Students: Read the parables outlined on page 89.

First Communicants: Complete "Day 67" in your First Communion journal.

Family Read Aloud: Read Chapter 19 in *The King of the Golden City*.

Narration
After reading, narrate the events of this chapter.

Parallel Figures Chart
training to come to an end, come in your disguise to the little hut

Discussion Topics
Describe the ways in which Dilecta trained Self. In what ways was Self becoming better behaved? In what ways does your Self need more training? List at least three ways that you can work with your Self in order to have him/her better trained. List too several ways in which you can try to know and love Jesus better. "Do not grow slack in zeal, be fervent in spirit, serve the Lord." (Romans 12:11)

Searching Scripture
Psalm 24, Psalm 122:1, Matthew 16:27, Mark 13:32-37, 2 Timothy 4:6-8, James 1:12, and 1 Peter 5:4

Growing in Holiness
Based upon the prayer of Dilecta as she viewed Jesus face-to-face, prepare a short prayer of thanksgiving for Jesus' presence in the Holy Eucharist. Recite this prayer either before receiving Communion or immediately after its reception.

Carmelite Connections
1. "Once our debts have been paid we shall be able to walk in safety. We shall not be going into a foreign land, but into our own country, for it belongs to Him Whom we have loved so truly and Who Himself loves us." (*Way of Perfection* XL.8)

2. "... I was weary of earthly pilgrimages and only longed for the beauties of Heaven." (*Story of a Soul*, Chapter VI)

3. "But how shall I show my love, since love proves itself by deeds? Well! The little child will strew flowers. . . . she will embrace the Divine Throne with their fragrance, she will sing Love's Canticle in silvery tones. Yes, my Beloved, it is thus my short life shall be spent in Thy sight. The only way I have of proving my love is to strew flowers before Thee—that is to say, I will let no tiny sacrifice pass, no look, no word. I wish to profit by the smallest actions, and to do them for Love. I wish to suffer for Love's sake, and for Love's sake even to rejoice: thus shall I strew flowers. Not one shall I find without scattering its petals before Thee . . . and I will sing. . . . I will sing always, even if my roses must be gathered from amidst thorns; and the longer and sharper the thorns, the sweeter shall be my song. But of what avail to thee, my Jesus, are my flowers and my songs? I know it well: this fragrant shower, these delicate petals of little price, these songs of love from a poor little heart like mine, will nevertheless be pleasing unto Thee. Trifles they are, but Thou wilt smile on them. The Church Triumphant, stooping towards her child, will gather up these scattered rose leaves, and, placing them in Thy Divine Hands, there to acquire an infinite value, will shower them on the Church Suffering to extinguish its flames, and on the Church Militant to obtain its victory." (*Story of a Soul*, Chapter XI)

4. "... it was folly to come and seek the poor hearts of mortal men to make them thrones for Him, the King of Glory, Who sits above the Cherubim! Was He not supremely happy in the company of His Father and the Holy Spirit of Love? Why, then, come down on earth to seek sinners and make of them His closest friends? Nay, our folly could never exceed His . . ." (*Story of a Soul*, Letter to Celine, XX)

5. "I seem already to touch the Heavenly Shore and to receive Our Lord's embrace. I fancy I can see Our Blessed Lady coming to meet me . . . and I picture myself enjoying true family joys for all eternity." (*Story of a Soul*, Chapter IV)

6. "... I never on any occasion saw more than the Lord was pleased to show me. What I saw was so great that the smallest part of it was sufficient to leave my soul amazed and to do it so much good that it esteemed and considered all the things of this life as of little worth. I wish I could give a description of at least the smallest part of what I learned, but, when I try to discover a way of doing so, I find it impossible; for, while the light we see here and that other light are both light, there is no comparison between the two and the brightness of the sun seems quite dull if compared with the other. In short, however skillful the imagination may be, it will not succeed in picturing or describing what that light is like, nor a single one of those things that I learned from the Lord with a joy so sovereign as to be indescribable. For all the senses rejoice in a high degree, and with a sweetness impossible to describe, for which reason it is better to say no more about it." (*Life of the Holy Mother Teresa of Jesus* XXXVIII.2)

7. "And thus this soul . . . at the gates of the palace . . . is recompensed . . . in a single day for all its trials and services, for not only is it made to enter the palace and stand before the King, clothed in regal vesture, but likewise it is crowned, and given a scepter,

and a royal seat, and possession of the royal ring, so that it may do all that it desires, and need do naught that it desires not to do in the kingdom of its Spouse; for those that are in this state receive all that they desire." (*Living Flame*, Second Redaction, II.31)

Optional Catechism Lessons
1. First Communicants should complete one of the following:
    a. Finish testing the memorization of catechism questions 1-54 as well as the Ten Commandments, the seven sacraments, and the prayers **or**
    b. Finish reviewing questions 1-42 in *Jesus Our Life* and the "Words to Know" on pages 141-147.
2. Death (*Book No. 2* only)

Friday, Week 10 (Day 68)

Parents: If possible, make a holy hour with the entire family in church to ask God to grant mercy and peace to each member of your family through the infinite merits gained by Jesus upon His death on the cross. Pray the Stations of the Cross together.

High School and Middle School Students: Read the meditations on pages 89-91.

First Communicants: Complete "Day 68" in your First Communion journal.

Family Read Aloud: See pages 93-96 for Pope St. Pius X's encyclical, "On Frequent and Daily Reception of Holy Communion," *Sacred Tridentina* (If all children are young, then parents may read this document and discuss it briefly with them.)

Complete the worksheets on pages 75-76. These exercises match the parts of the Mass with Scripture from the New American Bible translation. (An answer key for this exercises is provided on pages 131-132.)

Today and tomorrow, complete any unfinished reading assignments and weekend projects.

Saturday, Week 10 (Day 69)

Parents: If possible, make a holy hour with the entire family in church to ask Mary to always keep each member of your family close to her beloved Son. Recite the rosary together.

High School and Middle School Students: Read the meditational reading on pages 91-92.

First Communicants: Complete "Day 69" in your First Communion journal.

Family Read Aloud: See pages 97-101 for Pope St. Pius X's encyclical, "Decree on First Communion," *Quam Singulari*. (If all children are young, then parents may read this document and discuss it briefly with them.)

Matching Exercise on the Words of the Mass
(Revised for the new translation, November 2011)

Many of the words we pray at Mass are taken directly from the Bible, from both the Old and New Testaments. Below you will find—in two parts—the words we pray at Mass on the left and the matching Scriptural citation on the right. Draw a line from the words we speak to its proper citation on the right. Challenge yourself to find other references to Scripture in the words of the Mass.

Introductory Rites and Liturgy of the Word	Scriptural Citation
". . . in the name of the Father, and of the Son, and of the Holy Spirit."	2 Corinthians 9:15
"Amen."	Matthew 28:19
"The Lord be with you."	Luke 2:14
"And with your spirit."	Galatians 6:18
"I have greatly sinned . . ."	Luke 1:28
". . . and in what I have failed to do . . ."	James 4:17
"Glory to God in the highest . . ."	Revelation 5:14
"Lord Jesus Christ, Only Begotten Son . . ."	John 1:14
"You are seated at the right hand of the Father . . ."	Revelation 19:1-7
"Thanks be to God . . ."	1 Chronicles 21:8
"Alleluia."	Mark 16:19

Liturgy of the Eucharist and Concluding Rites

	Scriptural Citation
"Lift up your hearts."	Lamentations 3:41 and Colossians 3:1-2
"Holy, holy, holy . . ."	John 1:29
"While they were eating, he took bread . . . this is my body."	Isaiah 6:3
"When we eat this bread and drink this cup . . ."	Matthew 8:8
"Our Father . . ."	Matthew 21:9
". . . as we await the blessed hope and the coming of our Savior . . ."	Titus 2:13
"Lamb of God, who takes away the sins of the world"	Matthew 6:9-13
"Blessed is he who comes in the name of the Lord. Hosanna in the highest."	Romans 11:36
"Through him, with him, in him . . ."	1 Corinthians 11:26
"Peace be with you."	Matthew 26:26-28
"Lord, I am not worthy to have you enter under my roof . . ."	Luke 24:36 and Romans 15:33

In addition to the words of the Mass, many of our actions and practices at Mass are taken directly from the Bible. Draw a line from the action on the left to its corresponding biblical citation on the right.

Sign of the Cross	Exodus 30:17-21
Confessing Our Sins	Psalm 51:1-4
Asking for God's Mercy	Ezekiel 9:4-6
Homily (Explaining the Readings)	1 Timothy 2:1-4
Intercessory Prayer (Praying for the Needs of Others)	Nehemiah 8:8 and Mark 1:21-22
Washing of the Hands	James 5:16 and 1 Corinthians 11:27-28
Being Sent Forth to Proclaim the Gospel	John 20:21

Communion with the Saints,
A Family Preparation Program for First
Communion and Beyond in the Spirit of St. Therese

Reading Schedule for High School and Middle School Students

The reading selections through Day 51 are taken from *Divine Mercy in My Soul* and include "My Preparation for Holy Communion" (Paragraphs 1804-1828) by Sr. Maria Faustina of the Blessed Sacrament, Congregation of the Sisters of Our Lady of Mercy, Cracow, January 10, 1938. The words of Jesus to Sr. Faustina are typed in *Italics*. The number in parentheses after each passage indicates the text paragraph of the quotation. (Note that Sr. Faustina was declared a saint of the Church on April 30, 2000.)

These readings are short and are intended to inspire the soul to meditation. Begin to spend ten to fifteen minutes each day in silent communion with God. Ideally, these readings are to be read in front of the Blessed Sacrament ten to fifteen minutes before daily Mass begins. Alternatively, visit Jesus in the tabernacle at a different time of day. If neither of these options is available, kneel before the crucifix in your bedroom. *"When you reflect upon what I tell you in the depths of your heart, you profit more than if you had read many books. Oh, if souls would only want to listen to My voice when I am speaking in the depths of their hearts, they would reach the peak of holiness in a short time."* (Diary, 584)

Week 1, Saturday (Day 6)
I have come to understand many of God's mysteries. I have come to know that Holy Communion remains in me until the next Holy Communion. A vivid and clearly felt presence of God continues in my soul. The awareness of this plunges me into deep recollection, without the slightest effort on my part. My heart is a living tabernacle in which the living Host is reserved. I have never sought God in some far-off place, but within myself. It is in the depths of my own being that I commune with my God. (Diary, 1302)

Write for the benefit of religious souls that it delights Me to come to their hearts in Holy Communion. But if there is anyone else in such a heart, I cannot bear it and quickly leave that heart, taking with Me all the gifts and graces I have prepared for the soul. And the soul does not even notice My going. After some time, inner emptiness and dissatisfaction will come to her attention. Oh, if only she would turn to Me then, I would help her to cleanse her heart, and I would fulfill everything to her soul; but without her knowledge and consent, I cannot be the Master of her heart. (Diary, 1683)

Week 2, Sunday (Day 7)
After Communion today, Jesus told me how much He desires to come to human hearts. *I desire to unite Myself with human souls; My great delight is to unite Myself with souls. Know,*

my daughter, that when I come to a human heart in Holy Communion, My hands are full of all kinds of graces which I want to give to the soul. But souls do not even pay any attention to Me: they leave Me to Myself and busy themselves with other things. Oh, how sad I am that souls do not recognize Love! They treat me as a dead object. I answered Jesus, "O Treasure of my heart, the only object of my love and entire delight of my soul, I want to adore You in my heart as You are adored on the throne of Your eternal glory. My love wants to make up to You at least in part for the coldness of so great a number of souls. Jesus, behold my heart which is for You a dwelling place to which no one else has entry. You alone repose in it as in a beautiful garden . . . (Diary, 1385)

Week 2, Saturday (Day 13)

Oh, how painful it is to Me that souls so seldom unite themselves to Me in Holy Communion. I wait for souls, and they are indifferent toward Me. I love them tenderly and sincerely, and they distrust Me. I want to lavish My graces on them, and they do not want to accept them. They treat Me as a dead object, whereas My heart is full of love and mercy. In order that you may know at least some of My pain, imagine the most tender of mothers who has great love for her children, while those children spurn her love. Consider her pain. No one is in a position to console her. This is but a feeble image and likeness of My love. (Diary, 1447)

Week 3, Sunday (Day 14)

On one occasion, Jesus gave me to know that when I pray for intentions which people are wont to entrust to me, he is always ready to grant His graces, but souls do not always want to accept them: *My Heart overflows with great mercy for souls, and especially for poor sinners. If only they could understand that I am the best of Fathers to them and that it is for them that the Blood and Water flowed from My Heart as from a fount overflowing with mercy. For them I dwell in the tabernacle as King of Mercy. I desire to bestow My graces upon souls, but they do not want to accept them. You, at least, come to Me as often as possible and take those graces they do not want to accept. In this way you will console My Heart. Oh, how indifferent are souls to so much goodness, to so many proofs of love! My Heart drinks only of the ingratitude and forgetfulness of souls living in the world. They have time for everything, but they have no time to come to Me for graces . . .* (Diary, 367)

Week 3, Saturday (Day 20)

. . . Here are a few words from a conversation I had with the Mother Directress (Mary Joseph) toward the end of my novitiate: "Sister, let simplicity and humility be the characteristic traits of your soul. Go through this life like a little child, always trusting, always full of simplicity and humility, content with everything, happy in every circumstance. There, where others fear, you will pass calmly along, thanks to this simplicity and humility. Remember this, Sister, for your whole life: as waters flow from the mountains down into the valleys, so, too, do God's graces flow only into humble souls." (Diary, 55)

Week 4, Sunday (Day 21)

When I started the Holy Hour, I wanted to immerse myself in the agony of Jesus in the Garden of Olives. Then I heard a voice in my soul: *Meditate on the mystery of the Incarnation. And suddenly the Infant Jesus appeared before me, radiant with beauty.* He told me how much God is pleased with simplicity in a soul. *Although My greatness is beyond understanding, I commune only with those who are little. I demand of you a childlike spirit.*

I now see clearly how God acts through the confessor and how fruitfully He keeps His promises. Two weeks ago, my confessor told me to reflect upon this spiritual childhood. It was somewhat difficult at first, but my confessor, disregarding my difficulties, told me to continue to reflect upon spiritual childhood. "In practice, this spiritual childhood should manifest itself in this way: a child does not worry about the past or the future, but makes use of the present moment. I want to emphasize that spiritual childlikeness in you, Sister, and I place great stress upon it." I can see how God bows down to my confessor's wishes; He does not show Himself to me at this time as a Teacher in the fullness of His strength and human adulthood, but as a little Child. The God who is beyond all understanding stoops to me under the appearance of a little Child. (Diary, 332-333)

Week 4, Monday (Day 22)

Jesus, when You come to me in Holy Communion, you who together with the Father and the Holy Spirit have deigned to dwell in the little heaven of my heart, I try to keep You company throughout the day. I do not leave You alone for even a moment. Although I am in the company of other people or with our wards, my heart is always united to Him. When I am asleep I offer Him every beat of my heart; when I awaken I immerse myself in Him without saying a word. When I awaken I adore the Holy Trinity for a short while and thank God for having deigned to give me yet another day, that the mystery of the incarnation of His Son may once more be repeated in me, and that once again His sorrowful passion may unfold before my eyes. I then try to make it easier for Jesus to pass through me to other souls. I go everywhere with Jesus; His presence accompanies me everywhere. (Diary, 486)

Week 4, Tuesday (Day 23)

. . . Today, during Holy Mass, I saw the Crucified Jesus. Jesus was nailed to the cross and was in great agony. His suffering pierced me, soul and body, in a manner which was invisible, but nevertheless most painful.

Oh, what awesome mysteries take place during Mass! A great mystery is accomplished in the Holy Mass. With what great devotions should we listen to and take part in this death of Jesus. One day we will know what God is doing for us in each Mass, and what sort of gift He is preparing in it for us. Only His divine love could permit that such a gift be provided for us. O Jesus, my Jesus, with what great pain is my soul pierced when I see this fountain of life gushing forth with such sweetness and power for each soul, while at the same time I see souls withering away and drying up through their own fault. O Jesus, grant that the power of mercy embrace these souls. (Diary, 913-914)

Week 4, Wednesday (Day 24)

Silence is a sword in the spiritual struggle. A talkative soul will never attain sanctity. The sword of silence will cut off everything that would like to cling to the soul. We are sensitive to words and quickly want to answer back, without taking any regard as to whether it is God's will that we should speak. A silent soul is strong; no adversities will harm it if it perseveres in silence. The silent soul is capable of attaining closest union with God. It lives almost always under the inspiration of the Holy Spirit. God works in a silent soul without hindrance. (Diary, 477)

Week 4, Thursday (Day 25)

. . . the Holy Spirit does not speak to a soul that is distracted and garrulous [talking too much]. He speaks by His quiet inspirations to a soul that is recollected, to a soul that knows how to keep silence. (Diary, 552)

Patience, prayer and silence—these are what give strength to the soul. (Diary, 944)

Week 4, Friday (Day 26)

Jesus gave me to understand how a soul should be faithful to prayer despite torments, dryness and temptations; because oftentimes the realizations of God's great plans depends mainly on such prayer. If we do not persevere in such prayer, we frustrate what the Lord wanted to do through us or within us. Let every soul remember these words: 'And being in anguish, He prayed longer.' I always prolong such prayer as much as is in my power and conformity with my duty. (Diary, 872)

Week 4, Saturday (Day 27)

I have such a strong desire to hide myself that I would like to live as though I did not exist. I feel a strange desire to hide myself as deeply as possible so as to be known only to the Heart of Jesus. I want to be a quiet little dwelling place for Jesus to rest in. I shall admit nothing that might awaken my Beloved. My concealment gives me a chance to commune constantly and exclusively with my Bridegroom. I commune with creatures in so far as it is pleasing to Him. My heart has come to love the Lord with the full force of love, and I know no other love, because it is from the beginning that my soul has sunk deeply in the Lord as in its only treasure. (Diary, 1021)

Week 5, Sunday (Day 28)

Jesus, there is one more secret in my life, the deepest and dearest to my heart: it is You yourself when You come to my heart under the appearance of bread. Herein lies the whole secret of my sanctity. Here my heart is so united with yours as to be but one. There are no more secrets, because all that is Yours is mine, and all that is mine is Yours. Such is the omnipotence and the miracle of Your mercy. All the tongues of men and of angels united could not find words adequate to this mystery of Your love and mercy. (Diary, 1489)

Week 5, Monday (Day 29)

I became absorbed in prayer and said my penance. Then I suddenly saw the Lord, who said to me, *My daughter, know that you give Me greater glory by a single act of obedience than by long prayers and mortifications. Oh, how good it is to live under obedience, to live conscious of the fact that everything I do is pleasing to God!* (Diary, 894)

A single act of pure love pleases Me more than a thousand imperfect prayers. One of your sighs of love atones for many offenses with which the godless overwhelm Me. The smallest act of virtue has unlimited value in My eyes because of your great love for Me. In a soul that lives on My love alone, I reign as in heaven. I watch over it day and night. In it I find My happiness; My ear is attentive to each request of its heart; often I anticipate its requests. O child, especially beloved by Me, apple of My eye, rest a moment near My Heart and taste of the love in which you will delight for all eternity. (Diary, 1489)

Week 5, Tuesday (Day 30)

I adore You, Lord and Creator, hidden in the Blessed Sacrament. I adore You for all the works of Your hands that reveal to me so much wisdom, goodness and mercy, O Lord. You have spread so much beauty over the earth, and it tells me about Your beauty, even though these beautiful things are but a faint reflection of You, Incomprehensible Beauty. And although You have hidden Yourself and concealed Your beauty, my eye, enlightened by faith, reaches You, and my soul recognizes its Creator, its Highest Good; and my heart is completely immersed in prayer of adoration.

My Lord and Creator, Your goodness encourages me to converse with You. Your mercy abolishes the chasm which separates the Creator from the creature. To converse with You, O Lord, is the delight of my heart. In You I find everything that my heart could desire. Here Your light illumines my mind, enabling it to know You more and more deeply. Here streams of graces flow down upon my heart. Here my soul draws eternal life. O my Lord and Creator, You alone, beyond all these gifts, give your own self to me and unite yourself intimately with your miserable creature. Here, without searching for words, our hearts understand each other. Here, no one is able to interrupt our conversations. What I talk to You about, Jesus, is our secret, which creatures shall not know and angels dare not ask about. These are secret acts of forgiveness, known only to Jesus and me; this is the mystery of His mercy, which embraces each soul separately. For this incomprehensible goodness of Yours, I adore You, O Lord and Creator, with all my heart and all my soul. And, although my worship is so little and poor, I am at peace because I know that You know it is sincere, however inadequate . . . (Diary, 1692)

Week 5, Wednesday (Day 31)

O Everlasting Love, Jesus, who have enclosed Yourself in the Host, and therein hide Your divinity and conceal Your beauty, You do this in order to give Yourself, whole and entire, to my soul and in order not to terrify it with Your greatness. O Everlasting Love, Jesus, who have shrouded Yourself with bread, Eternal Light, incomprehensible Fountain of joy and happiness, because You want to be heaven on earth to me, that indeed You are, when Your love, O God, imparts itself to me. (Diary, 1569)

Week 5, Thursday (Day 32)

After Holy Communion, when I had welcomed Jesus into my heart, I said to Him, "My Love, reign in the most secret recesses of my heart, there where my most secret thoughts are conceived, where You alone have free access, in this deepest sanctuary where human thought cannot penetrate. May You alone dwell there, and may everything I do exteriorly take its origin in You. I ardently desire, and I am striving with all the strength of my soul, to make You, Lord, feel at home in this sanctuary." (Diary, 1721)

Week 5, Friday (Day 33)

My Jesus, how little these people talk about You. They talk about everything but You, Jesus. And if they talk so little (about You), it is quite probable that they do not think about You at all. The whole world interests them; but about You, their Creator, there is silence. Jesus, I am sad to see this great indifference and ingratitude of creatures. O my Jesus, I want to love You for them and to make atonement to You by my love. (Diary, 804)

Week 5, Saturday (Day 34)

On one occasion, I saw Satan hurrying about and looking for someone among the sisters, but he could find no one. I felt an interior inspiration to command him in the Name of God to confess to me what he was looking for among the sisters. And he confessed, though unwillingly, "I am looking for idle souls." (cf. Sirach 33:28; Proverbs 12:11) When I commanded him again in the Name of God to tell me to which souls in religious life he has the easiest access, he said, again unwillingly, "To lazy and idle souls." I took note of the fact that, at present, there were no such souls in this home. Let the toiling and tired souls rejoice. (Diary, 1127)

Week 6, Sunday (Day 35)

The Lord gave me to know how displeased He is with a talkative soul. I find no rest in such a soul. The constant din tires Me, and in the midst of it the soul cannot discern My voice. (Diary, 1008)

O life so dull and monotonous, how many treasures you contain! When I look at everything with the eyes of faith, no two hours are alike, and the dullness and monotony disappear. The grace which is given me in this hour will not be repeated in the next. It may be given me again, but it will not be the same grace. Time goes on, never to return again. Whatever is enclosed in it will never change; it seals with a seal for eternity. (Diary, 62)

Week 6, Monday (Day 36)

The most solemn moment of my life is the moment when I receive Holy Communion. I long for each Holy Communion, and for every Holy Communion. I give thanks to the Most Holy Trinity.

If the angels were capable of envy, they would envy us for two things: one is the receiving of Holy Communion, and the other is suffering. (Diary, 1804)

Today I am preparing myself for Your coming as a bride does for the coming of her bridegroom. He is a great Lord, this Bridegroom of mine. The heavens cannot contain Him. The Seraphim who stand closest to Him cover their faces and repeat unceasingly: Holy, Holy, Holy.

This great Lord is my Bridegroom. It is to Him that the Choirs sing. It is before Him that the Thrones bow down. By His splendor the sun is eclipsed. And yet this great Lord is my Bridegroom. My heart, desist from this profound meditation on how others adore Him, for you no longer have time for that, as He is coming and is already at your door.

I go out to meet Him, and I invite Him to the dwelling place of my heart, humbling myself profoundly before His majesty. But the Lord lifts me up from the dust and invites me, as His bride, to sit next to Him and to tell Him everything that is on my heart. And I, set at ease by His kindness, lean my head on His breast and tell Him of everything. In the first place, I tell Him things I would never tell to any creature. And then, I speak about the needs of the Church, about the souls of poor sinners and about how much they have need of His mercy. But the time passes quickly. Jesus, I must go to carry out the duties that are awaiting me. Jesus tells me that there is still a moment in which to say farewell. A deep mutual gaze, and we seemingly separate for a while; but, in reality, we never do. Our hearts are constantly united. Though outwardly I am distracted by my various duties, the presence of Jesus plunges me constantly in profound recollection. (Diary, 1805-1806)

Week 6, Tuesday (Day 37)
Today, my preparation for the coming of Jesus is brief, but imprinted deeply with vehement love. The presence of God penetrates me and sets aflame my love for Him. There are no words; there is only interior understanding. I drown completely in God, through love. The Lord approaches the dwelling of my heart. After receiving Communion, I have just enough presence of mind to return to my kneeler. At the same time, my soul is completely lost in God, and I no longer know what is going on about me. God gives me an interior knowledge of His Divine Being. These moments are short, but penetrating. The soul leaves the chapel in profound recollection, and it is not easy to distract it. At such times, I touch the ground with only one foot, as it were. No sacrifice throughout such a day is either difficult or burdensome. Every situation evokes a new act of love. (Diary, 1807)

Week 6, Wednesday (Day 38)
Today, I invite Jesus to my heart as Love. You are Love itself. All heaven catches the flame from You and is filled with love. And so my soul covets you as a flower yearns for the sun. Jesus, hasten to my heart, for You see that, as the flower is eager for the sun, so my heart is for You. I open the calyx of my heart to receive Your love.

When Jesus came to my heart, everything in my soul trembled with life and with warmth. Jesus, take the love from my heart and pour into it Your love, Your love which is burning and radiant, which knows how to bear each sacrifice, which knows how to forget itself completely.

Today, my day is marked by sacrifice . . . (Diary, 1808-1809)

Week 6, Thursday (Day 39)

Today, I prepare for the Coming of the King.

What am I, and who are You, O Lord, King of eternal glory? O my heart, are you aware of who is coming to you today? Yes, I know, but—strangely—I am not able to grasp it. Oh, if He were just a king, but He is the King of kings, the Lord of lords. Before Him, all power and dominion tremble. He is coming to my heart today. But I hear Him approaching. I go out to meet Him and invite Him. When he entered the dwelling of my heart, it was filled with such reverence that it fainted with fear, falling at His feet. Jesus gives her His hand and graciously permits her to take her place beside Him. He reassures her, saying, See, I have left My heavenly throne to become united with you. What you see is just a tiny part and already your soul swoons with love. How amazed will your heart be when you see Me in all My glory.

But I want to tell you that eternal life must begin already here on earth through Holy Communion. Each Holy Communion makes you more capable of communing with God throughout eternity.

And so, my King, I do not ask You for anything, although I know that You can give me everything. I ask You for one thing only: remain forever the King of my heart; that is enough for me.

Today I am renewing my act of submission to my King, by faithfulness to interior inspirations. (Diary, 1810-1812)

Week 6, Friday (Day 40)

Today, I am not forcing myself to make any special preparation. I cannot think of anything, though I feel many things. I long for the time when God will come to my heart. I throw myself in His arms and tell Him about my inability and my misery. I pour out all the pain of my heart, for not being able to love Him as much as I want. I arouse within myself acts of faith, hope, and charity and live on that throughout the day. (Diary, 1813)

Week 6, Saturday (Day 41)

Today, my preparation is brief. A strong and living faith nearly tears away the veil of love. The presence of God penetrates my heart as a ray from the sun penetrates crystal. At the moment when I receive God, all my being is steeped in Him. Amazement and admiration overwhelm me when I see God's great majesty, which stoops down to me who am misery itself. There bursts forth from my soul immense gratitude to Him for all the graces that He imparts to me, and especially for the grace of being called to His exclusive service. (Diary, 1814)

Week 7, Sunday (Day 42)

Today, in Holy Communion, I want to unite myself to Jesus as closely as possible, through love. I yearn for God so ardently that it seems to me that the moment will never come when the priest will give me Holy Communion. My soul falls as if into a swoon because of my longing for God.

When I received Him into my heart, the veil of faith was torn away. I saw Jesus who said to me, My daughter, your love compensates Me for the coldness of many souls. After these words, I was once again alone, but throughout the whole day I lived in an act of reparation. (Diary, 1815-1816)

Week 7, Monday (Day 43)
Today, I feel an abyss of misery in my soul. I want to approach Holy Communion as a fountain of mercy and to drown myself completely in this ocean of love. When I received Jesus, I threw myself into Him as into an abyss of unfathomable mercy. And the more I felt I was misery itself, the stronger grew my trust in Him. In this abasement, I passed the whole day. (Diary, 1817)

Week 7, Tuesday (Day 44)
Today, my soul has the disposition of a child. I unite myself to God as a child to its father. I feel completely like a child of God.

When I had received Holy Communion, I had a deeper knowledge of the heavenly Father and of His Fatherhood in relation to souls.

Today I live, glorifying the Holy Trinity. I thank God that he has deigned to adopt us as His children, through grace. (Diary, 1818-1819)

Week 7, Wednesday (Day 45)
Today, I want to be transformed, whole and entire, into the love of Jesus and to offer myself, together with Him, to the Heavenly Father.

During Holy Mass, I saw the Infant Jesus in the chalice and He said to me, *I am dwelling in your heart as you see Me in this chalice.*

After Holy Communion, I felt the beating of the heart of Jesus in my own heart. Although I have been aware, for a long time, that Holy Communion continues in me until the next Communion, today—and throughout the whole day—I am adoring Jesus in my heart and asking Him, by His grace, to protect little children from the evil that threatens them. A vivid and even physically felt presence of God continues throughout the day and does not in the least interfere with my duties. (Diary, 1820-1821)

Week 7, Thursday (Day 46)
Today, my soul desires to show, in a special way, its love to Jesus. When the Lord entered my heart, I threw myself down at His feet like a rosebud. I want the fragrance of my love to rise continually to the foot of Your throne. You see, Jesus, in this rosebud, all my heart [offered] to You, not only now when my heart is burning like a live coal, but also during the day, when I will give You proofs of my love by faithfulness to divine grace.

Today, all the difficulties and sufferings that I will encounter, I will quickly seize, like rosebuds, to throw at the feet of Jesus. Little matter that the hand, or rather the heart, bleeds . . . (Diary, 1822)

Week 7, Friday (Day 47)

Today, my soul is preparing for the coming of my Savior, who is goodness and love itself. Temptations and distractions torment me and do not let me prepare for the coming of the Lord. Therefore I desire even more ardently to receive You, Lord, because I know that when You come, You will rescue me from these torments. And if it is Your will that I should suffer, well then, fortify me for the struggle.

Jesus, Savior, who has deigned to come into my heart, drive away these distractions which are keeping me from talking to You.

Jesus answered me: *I want you to become like a knight experienced in battle, who can give orders to others amid the exploding shells. In the same way, My child, you should know how to master yourself amid the greatest difficulties, and let nothing drive you away from Me, not even your falls.*

Today I have been struggling all day long with a certain difficulty about which You, Jesus, know . . . (Diary, 1823)

Week 7, Saturday (Day 48)

Today, my heart trembles with joy. I desire very much that Jesus come to my heart. My longing heart is inflamed with an ever-increasing love.

When Jesus came, I threw myself into His arms like a little child. I told Him of my joy. Jesus listened to these outpourings of my love. When I asked pardon of Jesus for not preparing myself for Holy Communion, but for continually thinking of sharing in this joy as soon as possible, He answered that *Most pleasing to Me is this preparation with which you have received Me into your heart. Today, in a special way I bless this your joy. Nothing will disturb that joy throughout this day* . . . (Diary, 1824)

Week 8, Sunday (Day 49)

Today, my soul is preparing for the coming of the Lord, who can do all things, who can make me perfect and holy. I am preparing very carefully for His reception, but there arose the difficulty as to how to present this to Him? I rejected it [this difficulty] at once. I will present it as my heart dictates.

When I had received Jesus in Holy Communion, my heart cried out with all its might, "Jesus, transform me into another host! I want to be a living host for You. You are a great and all-powerful Lord; You can grant me this favor." And the Lord answered me, *You are a living host, pleasing to the Heavenly Father. But reflect: What is a host? A sacrifice. And so?*

O my Jesus, I understand the meaning of "host." the meaning of sacrifice. I desire to be before Your Majesty a living host; that is, a living sacrifice that daily burns in Your honor.

When my strength begins to fail, it is Holy Communion that will sustain me and give me strength. Indeed, I fear the day on which I will not receive Holy Communion. My soul draws astonishing strength from Holy Communion.

O living Host, light of my soul! (Diary, 1825-1826)

Week 8, Monday (Day 50)

Today, my soul is preparing for Holy Communion as for a wedding feast, wherein all the participants are resplendent with unspeakable beauty. And I, too, have been invited to this banquet, but I do not see that beauty within myself, only an abyss of misery. And although I do not feel worthy of sitting down to table, I will however slip under the table, at the feet of Jesus, and will beg for the crumbs that fall from the table. Knowing Your mercy, I therefore approach You, Jesus, for sooner will I run out of misery than will the compassion of Your Heart exhaust itself. That is why during this day I will keep arousing trust in the divine mercy. (Diary, 1827)

Week 8, Tuesday (Day 51)

Today, the Majesty of God is surrounding me. There is no way that I can help myself to prepare better. I am thoroughly enwrapped in God. My soul is being inflamed by His love. I only know that I love and am loved. That is enough for me. I am trying my best to be faithful throughout the day to the Holy Spirit and to fulfill His demands. I am trying my best for interior silence in order to be able to hear His voice . . . (Diary, 1828)

Week 8, Wednesday (Day 52)

(In conjunction with the study of *The King of the Golden City*, the daily readings will be the parables of Jesus from the Bible rather than mediations from *Divine Mercy in My Soul*. Remember that a parable is similar to an allegory. Jesus, like Mother Loyola, taught moral lessons by using comparisons. Alternatively—or additionally—older siblings and adults may read the "Carmelite Connections" as taken from the Carmelite Doctors of the Church.)

Today read Jesus' explanation of the purpose of His parables: Matthew 13:10-15 and Matthew 13: 34-35. Read too the Old Testament prophecy regarding the need to pass these parables on to the next generation: Psalm 78:1-8. Meditate upon how you can use this information when studying an allegory such as *The King of the Golden City* as well as in our study of the parables of Jesus and their application to our daily lives.

Week 8, Thursday (Day 53)

Read the parable with the theme of the power of prayer: the judge and the widow, Luke 18:1-8.

Week 8, Friday (Day 54)

Read the parables that have the theme of the abuse of God's grace: the wedding feast, Matthew 22:1-14; and the great supper, Luke 14:16-24. Read too the parable about doing the will of God: the two sons, Matthew 21:28-31.

Week 8, Saturday (Day 55)

This weekend read the parables that have the theme of the kingdom of God on earth: the mustard seed, Matthew 13:31-32 or Mark 4:30-32 or Luke 13:18-19; the yeast, Luke 13:20-21; and the treasure hidden in a field, Matthew 13:44.

Week 9, Sunday (Day 56)
Continue reading the parables regarding the kingdom of God on earth: the pearl of great value, Matthew 8:45-46; the net cast into the sea, Matthew 8:47-50; and the seed cast into the earth, Mark 4:26-29.

Week 9, Monday (Day 57)
Read the parables with the theme of working for God and for heaven: the parable of the talents, Matthew 25:14-30; and the parable of the pounds, Luke 19:11-27.

Week 9, Tuesday (Day 58)
Read the parables with the theme of God's patience in His dealings with sinners: the weeds among the wheat, Matthew 13:24-30, 36-43; and the barren fig tree, Luke 13:6-9.

Week 9, Wednesday (Day 59)
Read the parable that has the theme of the reward of working for God: the laborers in the vineyard, Matthew 20:1-16.

Week 9, Thursday (Day 60)
Read the parable with the theme of Christ's love for us: the Good Shepherd, John 10:1-18.

Week 9, Friday (Day 61)
Read the parables that have the theme of forgiveness: the unforgiving servant, Matthew 18:21-35; the prodigal son, Luke 15:11-32; and the forgiven debtors, Luke 7:40-43.

Week 9, Saturday (Day 62)
Read the parables that speak of Christ's love for sinners: the lost sheep, Matthew 18:12-14 or Luke 15:1-7; and the lost coin, Luke 15:8-10.

Week 10, Sunday (Day 63)
Read the parable that has the theme of receiving God's Word: the sower and the seed, Matthew 13:3-8, 18-23 or Mark 4:2-8, 13-20 or Luke 8:4-15. Read too about the rejection of Jesus: Matthew 21:33-45 or Mark 7:1-12 or Luke 20:9-19.

Week 10, Monday (Day 64)
Read the parable that has a theme of humility and pride: the Pharisee and the tax collector, Luke 18:9-14.

Week 10, Tuesday (Day 65)
Read the parables that deal with the theme of the good and bad use of riches: the dishonest steward, Luke 16:1-8; and the rich man and Lazarus, Luke 16:19-31.

Week 10, Wednesday (Day 66)
Read the parable that speaks about the love of our neighbor: the good Samaritan, Luke 10:29-37.

Week 10, Thursday (Day 67)
Read the parables that have the theme of watchfulness and preparation for the judgment: the faithful or unfaithful servant, Matthew 24:45-51 or Luke 12:35-38, 41-46; the ten virgins, Matthew 25:1-13; and the rich fool, Luke 12:16-21.

Week 10, Friday (Day 68)
(The mediations for the next two days are excerpted from Daniel Lord's *Christ in Me.*)

Thanksgiving on the Call of Christ

1. Lord Jesus, King and Savior of the world, once more I hear within me the blessed invitation which you repeat graciously and with such insistence: "Come help me in the conquest of the world." Since your calling of the Apostles that invitation has echoed in a million, million hearts. You could have carried out your program for the salvation of the world without help from anyone. But you do not work that way, dear Jesus. You want our partnership. You desire our help. You wish us to share your labors so that we may share your glory. You give us part in your campaign to insure our part in your victory.

Dear Lord, in physical reality you have come to me as my partner today. I hear your voice calling me to your side. I thank you for that repeated invitation.

2. To what do you invite me, Lord Jesus? To a share in the glorious work that brought you from heaven to your life upon earth and your later Eucharistic life in the tabernacle. You plan to save the world from evil. You campaign to make the earth a decent place where God's sons and daughters can live in safety and peace. You long for the happiness and the fullest and richest personal development of your children. You vision the complete establishment of your Father's Kingdom upon earth. To a share in that glorious program you once more invite me.

Again my deepest thanks, dear Savior and generous Conqueror. My part in the campaign must be ridiculously slight compared with yours. But you are good and generous to invite me, and I am most happy and grateful for your invitation.

3. Perhaps the thought of world conquest appalls and terrifies me, Lord Jesus. Who am I to share your campaign to re-conquer the world for the Trinity? How can I, one small and unimportant individual, do anything significant to insure the happiness of the human race? Yet even as I ask, I know the answer; I hear your consistent reply; beyond all else you ask me for the conquest of my own heart and soul. The small world within me, that is my field of battle and conquest. There I must plant your flag, which is the cross, and enthrone you as conquering King.

Even this small part, Lord Jesus, is a frightening assignment. I know the wild rebellion of my heart. I know how traitorous are my passions and how cowardly is my will. I feel within me the presence of spies and rebels. I remember how often I have surrendered my heart and soul to Satan, your relentless enemy.

Yet you are already in my soul, Lord Jesus. You have come this morning in Holy Communion, which is your gentle conquest. The work is almost done, if only I will permit it and accept it. Take my heart and soul, King of the world, and make them a part of your Kingdom forever.

4. But it is your desire that I help you conquer the wider world too. I must help you with souls. This partnership of Holy Communion guarantees my victory in your battle for souls. I must pray that souls be won for you. I must by my sweetness and charity, my example and my gracious understanding woo souls to your side. With your constant help and partnership, your dear presence and winsome example I must go to my work among souls, conquering them through love and service and devotion to your cause.

Dear Jesus, once more I consecrate to you the work I shall do for souls. Give that work victory. Give it success for the sake of your glorious cause.

5. So I kneel, Lord Jesus, and fold my hands. I place my folded hands between your hands, as did the loyal subjects of great kings. Close your hands over mine, King of the world, while I renew my dedication to your cause.

Accept me, Eucharistic King, as your devoted partner in your campaign for the winning of the world. I shall pray as you did, love as you did, labor as you did, expend myself as you did, that men and women may be won for their own happiness, that the world may know freedom from the captivity of Satan, and that the Kingdom of your Father may be established everywhere.

Take me, Lord Jesus. Help me with the conquest of my own heart. Give me strength to battle for you in the only warfare worthy of you and of those who love you. Amen.

Week 10, Saturday (Day 69)
Gratitude for the Nearness of My God

1. Lord Jesus present in the Eucharist and in my heart, it could easily be that I grow too accustomed to your blessings, too familiar with the generosity of your Sacred Heart. Each day I may, if I wish, receive Holy Communion. As often as I desire, I may drop into the chapel to speak with you. You are with me so constantly that I dread the thought that familiarity might breed contempt and the very lavishness of your generous gifts might make me forget to be grateful. So this morning I should like to think over with you the wonderful privilege it is to be born into this particular age. Whatever the individual blessings that you shower on other periods of history, this is the age of the Eucharist. This is the age when God is very near to us. This is the age into which I should have chosen to be born.

You arranged that blessing for me, dear Jesus, and I am grateful.

2. Let me think, Eucharistic King, of what it would have meant to be born under the Old Law. How far away God would have seemed! I should have found heaven closed, God's presence in the Temple fleeting and cloudlike. I might be aware of His presence in the universe, His creative and sustaining power, His providence, His gifts of nature. But He would have seemed a far-off God, sending His presents but withholding His presence. I should have sighed for a sight of His face, living by hope and a faith that had seen too miserable little of His goodness and His merciful love.

I should never have known the crib, the cross, and the meaning of Holy Communion.

My thanks, dear Savior, that you allowed me to be born into a happier age.

3. Blessed Savior of the world, sometimes I imagine that it would have been wonderful to live when you walked the earth. But would I even have seen you? I might perhaps have glimpsed you for a brief hour. From some distant point I might have listened and watched while you spoke upon the Mount. I might have been one of the crowd that milled about you when you worked your miracles.

Passing you in the street, I might have touched furtively the hem of your cloak, deeming this an incredible privilege. But any contact with you would have been fleeting. You were in one place at a time. Perhaps never should my path have crossed yours. You could be seen only briefly; for you came and went, giving no notice of your arrival, no warning of your departure.

Everything is different now. I can find you in any tabernacle in any land. I can approach you at any time of the day or night. Uncounted times in my life, not just once, I can hold you in closest association. Indeed I can possess you, not as one of a crowd of listeners or spectators, but as your personal friend, your host, your associate. What great good fortune is mine!

4. I might have been born, dear Jesus, in the period of infrequent Communion. I might have lived in an age when priests were few and it was not possible to hear Mass very frequently. I might have lived in the days when good people went to Holy Communion once or twice a month and even religious received you perhaps only twice a week. I should have longed then for daily Communion. I should have yearned to receive you at every Mass. And I should have been denied.

But I am living in the age of frequent Communion. I may receive you daily. No law or custom holds you from me. Only my own apathy or sin could keep you from me—or me from you. How great should be my gratitude!

5. So I have new reason for gratitude, Lord Jesus. Mine is a daily association with the Lord of the universe and the Savior of my soul. You are not only in one place; you are in uncounted places. No hour of the day but you can be reached for immediate help and consultation. You are in a thousand, thousand tabernacles. You are a part of the day's blessed routine.

But there is the peril, dear Jesus. We grow slovenly in the face of favors. We become ungrateful if the Giver is too generous. We accept as routine what should be a constant wonder and amazement.

Keep me in this constant wonder, dear Jesus, at your presence and your generosity. Make each Holy Communion a lovely and individual event. Give me the grace of deep gratitude for your generosity that allows me to live in an age when you are so close, so dear, and so companionable. Amen.

Continue to spend some quiet time with God daily. Each and every day—including weekends—unite yourself with God in silence for ten to fifteen minutes. In our noisy world, learn to value silence.

If devotional material is needed to help direct your daily meditation time, use readings from the Gospels or obtain a copy of *Divine Mercy in My Soul*. This book, along with several other books on Divine Mercy for children and adults alike, is available from the publisher Marian Press—the printing arm of the Marian Helpers—by calling toll free at 1-800-462-7426. For more information on St. Faustina—including St. Faustina's "Revelation of the Day," or short daily readings from her work in *Mercy Minutes*—devotion to the Divine Mercy, or the Association of Marian Helpers (including their quarterly Bulletin), view their web site at www.marian.org.

Sacra Tridentina,
On Frequent and Daily Reception of Holy Communion
Issued and Approved by Pope Pius X on December 20, 1905

The Holy Council of Trent, having in view the ineffable riches of grace which are offered to the faithful who receive the Most Holy Eucharist, makes the following declaration: "The Holy Council wishes indeed that at each Mass the faithful who are present should communicate, not only in spiritual desire, but sacramentally, by the actual reception of the Eucharist." These words declare plainly enough the wish of the Church that all Christians should be daily nourished by this heavenly banquet and should derive there from more abundant fruit for their sanctification.

This wish of the Council fully conforms to that desire wherewith Christ our Lord was inflamed when He instituted this Divine Sacrament. For He Himself, more than once, and in clarity of word, pointed out the necessity of frequently eating His Flesh and drinking His Blood, especially in these words: This is the bread that has come down from heaven; not as your fathers ate the manna, and died. He who eats this bread shall live forever. From this comparison of the Food of angels with bread and with manna, it was easily to be understood by His disciples that, as the body is daily nourished with bread, and as the Hebrews were daily fed with manna in the desert, so the Christian soul might daily partake of this heavenly bread and be refreshed thereby. Moreover, we are bidden in the Lord's Prayer to ask for "our daily bread" by which words, the holy Fathers of the Church all but unanimously teach, must be understood not so much that material bread which is the support of the body as the Eucharistic bread which ought to be our daily food.

Moreover, the desire of Jesus Christ and of the Church that all the faithful should daily approach the sacred banquet is directed chiefly to this end, that the faithful, being united to God by means of the Sacrament, may thence derive strength to resist their sensual passions, to cleanse themselves from the stains of daily faults, and to avoid these graver sins to which human frailty is liable; so that its primary purpose is not that the honor and reverence due to our Lord may be safeguarded, or that it may serve as a reward or recompense of virtue bestowed on the recipients. Hence the Holy Council calls the Eucharist "the antidote whereby we may be freed from daily faults and be preserved from mortal sin."

The will of God in this respect was well understood by the first Christians; and they daily hastened to this Table of life and strength. They continued steadfastly in the teaching of the apostles and in the communion of the breaking of the bread. The holy Fathers and writers of the Church testify that this practice was continued into later ages and not without great increase of holiness and perfection.

Piety, however, grew cold, and especially afterward because of the widespread plague of Jansenism, disputes began to arise concerning the dispositions with which one ought to receive frequent and daily Communion; and writers vied with one another in demanding more and more stringent conditions as necessary to be fulfilled. The result of such disputes was that very few were considered worthy to receive the Holy Eucharist daily, and to derive from this most health-giving Sacrament its more abundant fruits; the others were content to partake of it once a year, or once a month, or at most once a week. To such a degree, indeed, was rigorism carried that whole classes of persons were excluded from a frequent approach to the Holy Table, for instance, merchants or those who were married.

Some, however, went over to the opposite view. They held that daily Communion was prescribed by divine law and that no day should pass without communicating, and besides other practices not in accord with the approved usage of the Church, they determined that the Eucharist must be received even on Good Friday and in fact so administered it.

Toward these conditions, the Holy See did not fail in its duty. A Decree of this Sacred Congregation which begins with the words *Cum ad aures*, issued on February 12, 1679, with the approbation of Pope Innocent XI, condemned these errors, and put a stop to such abuses; at the same time it declared that all the faithful of whatsoever class, merchants or married persons not at all excepted, could be admitted to frequent Communion according to the devotion of each one and the judgment of his confessor. Then on December 7, 1690, by the Decree of Pope Alexander VIII, *Sanctissimus Dominus Noster*, the proposition of Baius was condemned, requiring a most pure love of God, without any admixture of defect, on the part of those who wished to approach the Holy Table.

The poison of Jansenism, however, which, under the pretext of showing due honor and reverence to the Eucharist, had infected the minds even of good men, was by no means a thing of the past. The question as to the dispositions for the proper and licit reception of Holy Communion survived the declarations of the Holy See, and it was a fact that certain theologians of good repute were of the opinion that daily Communion could be permitted to the faithful only rarely and subject to many conditions.

On the other hand, there were not wanting men endowed with learning and piety who offered an easier approach to this practice, so salutary and so pleasing to God. They taught, with the authority of the Fathers, that there is no precept of the Church which prescribes more perfect dispositions in the case of daily than of weekly or monthly Communion; while the fruits of daily Communion will be far more abundant than those of Communion received weekly or monthly.

In our own day the controversy has been continued with increased warmth, and not without bitterness, so that the minds of confessors and the consciences of the faithful have been disturbed, to the no small detriment of Christian piety and fervor. Certain distinguished men, themselves pastors of souls, have as a result of this, urgently begged His Holiness, Pope Pius X, to design to settle, by his supreme authority, the question concerning the dispositions required to receive the Eucharist daily; so that this practice, so salutary and so pleasing to God, not only might suffer no decrease among the faithful, but rather that it increase and everywhere be promoted, especially in these days when religion and the Catholic faith are attacked on all sides, and the true love of God and piety are so frequently lacking. His Holiness, being most earnestly desirous, out of his solicitude and zeal, that the faithful should be invited to the sacred banquet as often as possible, even daily, and should benefit by its most abundant fruits, committed this question to this Sacred Congregation, to be studied and decided definitely (*definiendam*).

Accordingly, the Sacred Congregation of the Council, in a Plenary Session held on December 16, 1905, submitted this matter to a very careful study, and after sedulously examining the reasons adduced on either side, determined and declared as follows:

1. Frequent and daily Communion, as a practice most earnestly desired by Christ our Lord and by the Catholic Church, should be open to all the faithful, of whatever rank and condition of life; so that no one who is in the state of grace, and who approaches the Holy Table with a right and devout intention (*recta piaque mente*) can be prohibited therefrom.

2. A right intention consists in this: that he who approaches the Holy Table should do so, not out of routine, or vain glory, or human respect, but that he wish to please God, to be more closely united with Him by charity, and to have recourse to this divine remedy for his weakness and defects.

3. Although it is especially fitting that those who receive Communion frequently or daily should be free from venial sins, at least from such as are fully deliberate, and from any affection thereto, nevertheless, it is sufficient that they be free from mortal sin, with the purpose of never sinning in the future; and if they have this sincere purpose, it is impossible by that daily communicants should gradually free themselves even from venial sins, and from all affection thereto.

4. Since, however, the Sacraments of the New Law, though they produce their effect *ex opere operato*, nevertheless, produce a great effect in proportion as the dispositions of the recipient are better, therefore, one should take care that Holy Communion be preceded by careful preparation, and followed by an appropriate thanksgiving, according to each one's strength, circumstances and duties.

5. That the practice of frequent and daily Communion may be carried out with greater prudence and more fruitful merit, the confessor's advice should be asked. Confessors, however, must take care not to dissuade anyone from frequent or daily Communion, provided he is found to be in a state of grace and approaches with a right intention.

6. But since it is plain that by the frequent or daily reception of the Holy Eucharist union with Christ is strengthened, the spiritual life more abundantly sustained, the soul more richly endowed with virtues, and the pledge of everlasting happiness more securely bestowed on the recipient, therefore, parish priests, confessors and preachers, according to the approved teaching of the Roman Catechism should exhort the faithful frequently and with great zeal to this devout and salutary practice.

7. Frequent and daily Communion is to be promoted especially in religious Institutes of all kinds; with regard to which, however, the Decree *Quemadmodum* issued on December 17, 1890, by the Sacred Congregation of Bishops and Regulars, is to remain in force. It is to be promoted especially in ecclesiastical seminaries, where siblings are

preparing for the service of the altar; as also in all Christian establishments which in any way provide for the care of the young (*ephebeis*).

8. In the case of religious Institutes, whether of solemn or simple vows, in whose rules, or constitutions, or calendars, Communion is assigned to certain fixed days, such regulations are to be considered as directive and not preceptive. The prescribed number of Communions should be regarded as a minimum but not a limit to the devotion of the religious. Therefore, access to the Eucharistic Table, whether it be rather frequently or daily, must always be freely open to them according to the norms above laid down in this Decree. Furthermore, in order that all religious of both sexes may clearly understand the prescriptions of this Decree, the Superior of each house will provide that it be read in community, in the vernacular, every year within the octave of the Feast of Corpus Christi.

9. Finally, after the publication of this Decree, all ecclesiastical writers are to cease from contentious controversy concerning the dispositions requisite for frequent and daily Communion.

All this having been reported to His Holiness, Pope Pius X, by the undersigned Secretary of the Sacred Congregation in an audience held on December 17, 1905, His Holiness ratified this Decree, confirmed it and ordered its publication, anything to the contrary notwithstanding. He further ordered that it should be sent to all local Ordinaries and regular prelates, to be communicated by them to their respective seminaries, parishes, religious institutes, and priests; and that in their report on the state of their dioceses or institutes they should inform the Holy See concerning the execution of the prescriptions therein enacted.

Given at Rome, the 20th day of December, 1905
(Excerpted from the Eternal Word Television Network online library at: www.ewtn.com/library/CURIA/CDWFREQ.HTM)

Quam Singulari, Decree on First Communion
Sacred Congregation of the Discipline of the Sacraments
August 8, 1910

The pages of the Gospel show clearly how special was that love for children which Christ showed while He was on earth. It was His delight to be in their midst; He was wont to lay His hands on them; He embraced them; and He blessed them. At the same time He was not pleased when they would be driven away by the disciples, whom He rebuked gravely with these words: "Let the little children come to me, and do not hinder them, for of such is the kingdom of God." It is clearly seen how highly He held their innocence and the open simplicity of their souls on that occasion when He called a little child to Him and said to the disciples: "Again, I say to you, unless you turn and become like little children, you will not enter into the kingdom of heaven....And whoever receives one such little child for my sake, receives me."

The Catholic Church, bearing this in mind, took care even from the beginning to bring the little ones to Christ through Eucharistic Communion, which was administered even to nursing infants. This, as was prescribed in almost all ancient Ritual books, was done at Baptism until the thirteenth century, and this custom prevailed in some places even later. It is still found in the Greek and Oriental Churches. But to remove the danger that infants might eject the Consecrated Host, the custom obtained from the beginning of administering the Eucharist to them under the species of wine only. Infants, however, not only at the time of Baptism, but also frequently thereafter were admitted to the sacred repast. In some churches it was the custom to give the Eucharist to the children immediately after the clergy; in others, the small fragments which remained after the Communion of the adults were given to the children.

This practice later died out in the Latin Church, and children were not permitted to approach the Holy Table until they had come to the use of reason and had some knowledge of this august Sacrament. This new practice, already accepted by certain local councils, was solemnly confirmed by the Fourth Council of the Lateran, in 1215, which promulgated its celebrated Canon XXI, whereby sacramental Confession and Holy Communion were made obligatory on the faithful after they had attained the use of reason, in these words: "All the faithful of both sexes shall, after reaching the years of discretion, make private confession of all their sins to their own priest at least once a year, and shall, according to their capacity, perform the enjoined penance; they shall also devoutly receive the Sacrament of Holy Eucharist at least at Easter time unless on the advice of their own priest, for some reasonable cause, it be deemed well to abstain for a while."

The Council of Trent, in no way condemning the ancient practice of administering the Eucharist to children before they had attained the use of reason, confirmed the Decree of the Lateran Council and declared anathema those who held otherwise: "If anyone denies that each and all Christians of both sexes are bound, when they have attained the years of discretion, to receive Communion every year at least at Easter, in accordance with the precept of Holy Mother Church, let him be anathema."

In accord with this Decree of the Lateran Council, still in effect, the faithful are obliged, as soon as they arrive at the years of discretion, to receive the Sacraments of Penance and Holy Eucharist at least once a year.

However, in the precise determination of "the age of reason or discretion" not a few errors and deplorable abuses have crept in during the course of time. There were some who maintained that one age of discretion must be assigned to reception of the Sacrament of Penance and another to the Holy Eucharist. They held that for Confession the age of discretion is reached when one can distinguish right from wrong, hence can commit sin; for Holy Eucharist, however, a greater age is required in which a full knowledge of matters of faith and a better preparation of the soul can be had. As a consequence, owing to various local customs and opinions, the age determined for the reception of First Communion was placed at ten years or twelve, and in places fourteen years or even more were required; and until that age children and youth were prohibited from Eucharistic Communion.

This practice of preventing the faithful from receiving on the plea of safeguarding the august Sacrament has been the cause of many evils. It happened that children in their innocence were forced away from the embrace of Christ and deprived of the food of their interior life; and from this it also happened that in their youth, destitute of this strong help, surrounded by so many temptations, they lost their innocence and fell into vicious habits even before tasting of the Sacred Mysteries. And even if a thorough instruction and a careful Sacramental Confession should precede Holy Communion, which does not everywhere occur, still the loss of first innocence is always to be deplored and might have been avoided by reception of the Eucharist in more tender years.

No less worthy of condemnation is that practice which prevails in many places prohibiting from Sacramental Confession children who have not yet made their First Holy Communion, or of not giving them absolution. Thus it happens that they, perhaps having fallen into serious sin, remain in that very dangerous state for a long time.

But worse still is the practice in certain places which prohibits children who have not yet made their First Communion from being fortified by the Holy Viaticum, even when they are in imminent danger of death; and thus, when they die they are buried with the rites due to infants and are deprived of the prayers of the Church.

Such is the injury caused by those who insist on extraordinary preparations for First Communion, beyond what is reasonable; and they doubtless do not realize that such precautions proceed from the errors of the Jansenists who contended that the Most Holy Eucharist is a reward rather than a remedy for human frailty. The Council of Trent, indeed, teaches otherwise when it calls the Eucharist, "An antidote whereby we may be freed from daily faults and be preserved from mortal sins." This doctrine was not long ago strongly emphasized by a Decree of the Sacred Congregation of the Council given on December 20, 1905. It declared that daily approach to Communion is open to all, old and young, and two conditions only are required: the state of grace and a right intention.

Moreover, the fact that in ancient times the remaining particles of the Sacred Species were even given to nursing infants seems to indicate that no extraordinary preparation should now be demanded of children who are in the happy state of innocence and purity of soul, and who, amidst so many dangers and seductions of the present time have a special need of this heavenly food.

The abuses which we are condemning are due to the fact that they who distinguished one age of discretion for Penance and another for the Eucharist did so in error. The Lateran Council required one and the same age for reception of either Sacrament when it imposed the one obligation of Confession and Communion.

Therefore, the age of discretion for Confession is the time when one can distinguish between right and wrong, that is, when one arrives at a certain use of reason, and so similarly, for Holy Communion is required the age when one can distinguish between the Bread of the Holy Eucharist and ordinary bread—again the age at which a child attains the use of reason.

The principal interpreters of the Lateran Council and contemporaries of that period had the same teaching concerning this Decree. The history of the Church reveals that a number of synods and episcopal decrees beginning with the twelfth century, shortly after the Lateran Council, admitted children of seven years of age to First Communion. There is moreover the word of St. Thomas Aquinas, who is an authority of the highest order, which reads: "When children begin to have some use of reason, so that they can conceive a devotion toward this Sacrament (the Eucharist), then this Sacrament can be given to them." Ledesma thus explains these words: "I say, in accord with common opinion, that the Eucharist is to be given to all who have the use of reason, and just as soon as they attain the use of reason, even though at the time the child may have only a confused notion of what he is doing." Vasquez comments on the same words of St. Thomas as follows: "When a child has once arrived at the use of reason he is immediately bound by the divine law from which not even the Church can dispense him."

The same is the teachings of St. Antoninus, who wrote: "But when a child is capable of doing wrong, that is of committing a mortal sin, then he is bound by the precept of Confession and consequently of Communion." The Council of Trent also forces us to the same conclusion when it declares: "Children who have not attained the use of reason are not by any necessity bound to Sacramental Communion of the Eucharist." It assigns as the only reason the fact that they cannot commit sin: "They cannot at that age lose the grace of the sons of God already acquired."

From this it is the mind of the Council that children are held to Communion by necessity and by precept when they are capable of losing grace by sin. The words of the Roman Synod, held under Benedict XIII, are in agreement with this in teaching that the obligation to receive the Eucharist begins, "After boys and girls attain the age of discretion, that is, at the age in which they can distinguish this Sacramental food, which is none other than the true Body of Jesus Christ, from common and ordinary bread; and that they know how to receive it with proper religious spirit."

The Roman Catechism adds this: "At what age children are to receive the Holy Mysteries no one can better judge than their father and the priest who is their confessor. For it is their duty to ascertain by questioning the children whether they have any understanding of this admirable Sacrament and if they have any desire for it."

From all this it is clear that the age of discretion for receiving Holy Communion is that at which the child knows the difference between the Eucharistic Bread and ordinary, material bread, and can therefore approach the altar with proper devotion. Perfect knowledge of the things of faith, therefore, is not required, for an elementary knowledge suffices—some knowledge (*aliqua cognitio*); similarly full use of reason is not required, for a certain beginning of the use of reason, that is, some use of reason (*aliqualis usus rationis*) suffices.

To postpone Communion, therefore, until later and to insist on a more mature age for its reception must be absolutely discouraged, and indeed such practice was condemned more than once by the Holy See. Thus Pope Pius IX, of happy memory, in a Letter of Cardinal Antonelli to the Bishops of France, March 12, 1866, severely condemned the growing custom existing in some dioceses of postponing the First Communion of children until more mature years, and at the same time sharply disapproved of the age limit which had been assigned. Again, the Sacred Congregation of the Council, on March 15, 1851, corrected a prescription of the Provincial Council of Rouen, which prohibited children under twelve years of age from receiving First Communion. Similarly, this Sacred Congregation of the Discipline of the Sacraments, on March 25, 1910, in a question proposed to it from Strasburg whether children of twelve or fourteen years could be admitted to Holy Communion, answered: "Boys and girls are to be admitted to the Holy Table when they arrive at the years of discretion or the use of reason."

After careful deliberation on all these points, this Sacred Congregation of the Discipline of the Sacraments, in a general meeting held on July 15, 1910, in order to remove the above-mentioned abuses and to bring about that children even from their tender years may be united to Jesus Christ, may live His life, and obtain protection from all danger of corruption, has deemed it needful to prescribe the following rules which are to be observed everywhere for the First Communion of children.

1. The age of discretion, both for Confession and for Holy Communion, is the time when a child begins to reason, that is about the seventh year, more or less. From that time on begins the obligation of fulfilling the precept of both Confession and Communion.

2. A full and perfect knowledge of Christian doctrine is not necessary either for First Confession or for First Communion. Afterwards, however, the child will be obliged to learn gradually the entire Catechism according to his ability.

3. The knowledge of religion which is required in a child in order to be properly prepared to receive First Communion is such that he will understand according to his capacity those Mysteries of faith which are necessary as a means of salvation (*necessitate medii*) and that he can distinguish between the Bread of the Eucharist and ordinary, material

bread, and thus he may receive Holy Communion with a devotion becoming his years.

4. The obligation of the precept of Confession and Communion which binds the child particularly affects those who have him in charge, namely, parents, confessor, teachers and the pastor. It belongs to the father, or the person taking his place, and to the confessor, according to the Roman Catechism, to admit a child to his First Communion.

5. The pastor should announce and hold a General Communion of the children once a year or more often, and he should on these occasions admit not only the First Communicants but also others who have already approached the Holy Table with the above-mentioned consent of their parents or confessor. Some days of instruction and preparation should be previously given to both classes of children.

6. Those who have charge of the children should zealously see to it that after their First Communion these children frequently approach the Holy Table, even daily if possible, as Jesus Christ and Mother Church desire, and let this be done with a devotion becoming their age. They must also bear in mind that very grave duty which obliged them to have the children attend the public Catechism classes; if this is not done, then they must supply religious instruction in some other way.

7. The custom of not admitting children to Confession or of not giving them absolution when they have already attained the use of reason must be entirely abandoned. The Ordinary shall see to it that this condition ceases absolutely, and he may, if necessary, use legal measures accordingly.

8. The practice of not administering the Viaticum and Extreme Unction to children who have attained the use of reason, and of burying them with the rite used for infants is a most intolerable abuse. The Ordinary should take very severe measures against those who do not give up the practice.

His Holiness, Pope Pius X, in an audience granted on the seventh day of this month, approved all the above decisions of this Sacred Congregation, and ordered this Decree to be published and promulgated.

He furthermore commanded that all the Ordinaries make this Decree known not only to the pastors and the clergy, but also to the people, and he wishes that it be read in the vernacular every year at the Easter time. The Ordinaries shall give an account of the observance of this Decree together with other diocesan matters every five years.

(The above document was taken from the Eternal Word Television Network web site at: www.ewtn.com/library/CURIA/CDWFIRST.HTM.)

Psalms for Holy Communion

Although many passages from Scripture could be used, the following readings—including readings from the book of Psalms as well as one passage each from the *Catechism of the Catholic Church* and the book of Daniel—are appropriate for use in either our preparation for or thanksgiving of Holy Communion. Memorize your favorites.

Preparation for Holy Communion	Thanksgiving of Holy Communion
Psalm 15 – The Guest of God	Psalm 34 – Praise of God
Psalm 23 – The Lord Is My Shepherd	Psalm 66 – Praise of God
Psalm 24 – The Lord's Entry into Zion	Psalm 81 Festive Song
Psalm 25 – Prayer for Guidance and Help	Psalm 91 – Security Under God's Protection
Psalm 26 – Prayer of an Innocent Man	Psalm 96 – The Glories of the Lord
Psalm 51 – Prayer of Repentance	Psalm 98 – The Lord, Victorious King
Psalm 63 – Ardent Longing for God	Psalm 103 – Praise of Divine Goodness
Psalm 84 – Desire for the Sanctuary	Psalm 111 – Praise of God for His Goodness
Psalm 85 – Prayer for Complete Restoration	Psalm 113 – Praise of the Lord for His Care of the Lowly
Psalm 116 – Thanksgiving to God for Help	Psalm 117 – Doxology of All the Nations
Psalm 130 – Prayer for Pardon and Mercy	Psalm 118 – Hymn of Thanksgiving
Psalm 132 – Pact between David and the Lord	Psalm 121 – The Lord Our Guardian Psalm 126 – People's Prayer Psalm 134 – Exhortation to the Night Watch to Bless the Lord Psalm 138 – Hymn of a Grateful Heart
Also be sure to read text paragraphs 1384-1390 in the *Catechism of the Catholic Church*	Psalm 145 – The Greatness and Goodness of God
	Psalm 146 – Trust in God Alone
	Psalm 147 – Zion's Grateful Praise
	Psalm 148 – Hymn of All Creation
	Psalm 149 – Invitation to Glorify the Lord with Song and Sword
	Psalm 150 – Final Doxology
	Daniel 3:52-88 – Canticle of the Three Young Men

Communion with the Saints, A Family Preparation Program for First Communion and Beyond in the Spirit of St. Therese

Weekend Projects

General Instructions

The following projects range from crafts and field trips to the establishment of family customs. Some projects are outlined in general terms only, leaving room for each family to creatively customize the project. Projects are grouped according to category with those projects that can be completed at home listed first followed by projects that require travel or activity outside the home. Listed last are those projects that are long-term or ongoing projects. All of the projects are listed on the summary chart found on page 112 below.

One family project should be completed each weekend. As thirty-eight separate project ideas are provided within this manual, there are plenty from which to choose. Weekdays are filled with readings, meditation time, written and oral exercises, and religious study. Weekends should be devoted to spending time as a family in establishing a Catholic culture within your home and throughout your family practices. Remember too to "keep holy the Sabbath"—attend Mass, reflect on the good God's great gifts, and rejoice with each other in His Presence!

Home Projects

1. Using felt or poster board, create a Eucharistic poster or banner to display on the anniversaries of each family member's First Holy Communion. Or create a baptismal banner or poster to display on the anniversary of each family member's baptismal day. Celebrate these feast days as you would birthdays—a special meal, special treats and/or small gifts. On the baptismal day, be sure to renew your baptismal promises (A plenary indulgence is attached with the usual norms.) and light your baptismal candle. (See the "Long-Term Projects" section below for more information on celebrating Catholic feasts and the liturgical year within your family.)

2. Prepare a family coat of arms. Include symbols regarding family ancestry, family values, occupations, and/or hobbies. Be sure to include at least one symbol or motto that makes a statement regarding your relationship to Jesus Christ.

3. Have your family consecrate themselves to the Sacred Heart of Jesus. Enthrone a picture of the Sacred Heart in a place of honor in your home. Pray a consecration prayer to the Sacred Heart daily, and renew this dedication each First Friday or yearly.

4. Research various saints. Find an appropriate patron saint for your family. Have a special celebration on that saint's feast day each year. Adopt the saint's motto or create your own family motto using a quotation of the saint's or one from Holy Scripture.

Obtain a holy card or frame a picture of this saint. Using embroidery, cross-stitching, calligraphy, or woodworking, give your motto a prominent place in your home.

5. Read together Fr. John Hardon's book, *With Us Today, On the Real Presence of Jesus Christ in the Eucharist*. This is an exceptional book.

6. Create a chart of family "Rules for Peaceful Living." Decide upon a code word to be used as a gentle reminder for any offenders. Establish a set of rewards for keeping these rules as well as a set of consequences. The rewards and consequences can be for individuals or for the family as a unit—such a family movie night as a reward for a week of truly peaceful living. Use Holy Scripture or the catechism for examples of appropriate rules.

7. Study the persecution of practicing Christians in the world today. We live in an age of martyrdom; more Christians died for their faith in the twentieth century than in the previous nineteen centuries combined. The World Christian Encyclopedia states that in 1998 close to 156,000 Christians were killed for their religious beliefs; in 1999 that figure rose to 164,000 and in 2000 an estimated 165,000 Christians were martyred. Using the Internet, research the 20th century persecution of Christians especially in Sudan, China, Mexico, Nazi Europe, Spain (during the civil war), the Soviet Empire, and Vietnam. How can each of us personally prepare for possible persecution and martyrdom to help ensure that we will never deny Christ? What statistics can you find for the 21st century?

8. Put together a family photo album. One album for the entire family could be completed, or one album per child can be completed and added to as necessary. A special "Our Life in Christ" album can also be created to hold memories of family members' participation in Church activities, sacraments, baptismal celebrations, Lenten activities, feast days, etc. As an alternative, create a family scrapbook or a scrapbook for individual family members. Establish a regular time when these books will be updated—monthly or seasonally—as well as a time when they will be "read"—perhaps New Year's Eve or on each child's baptismal day. Remember that the family is the domestic Church and needs nurturing.

9. Taking the theological virtues of faith, hope, and love and adding to them the nine fruits of the Holy Spirit as outlined in Galatians 5:22, begin to study one of these per month. Read relevant Scripture verses or quotations from the saints. Emphasize the practice of this virtue and reward its observance in other family members. Two books may be helpful to follow this routine: *The 12 Steps to Holiness and Salvation* (from the works of St. Alphonsus Liguori) by Tan Books and Publishers, and *Spiritual Diary, Selected Sayings and Examples of Saints* by St. Paul Media. Both of these books provide one virtue to practice each month, with the former giving a general reading of the virtue and the latter providing daily readings for each month.

10. Could someone tell upon entering your home that you are a Catholic family? Make sure your home is a Catholic home. Remove any pictures or other decorations that are not pleasing to God—don't forget the bedrooms! Obtain some Catholic home decorations, such as a holy water font, Catholic saints' pictures and statutes, crucifixes

(one for the living area and one for each bedroom), pictures of the Sacred Heart of Jesus and the Immaculate Heart of Mary, a Divine Mercy picture, a large family Bible, a display rack for your rosaries and prayer books, a Catholic calendar, and perhaps even an outdoor Catholic shrine to proclaim your faith to passersby. Consider establishing a family altar with candles, a crucifix, statutes, and pictures. Does your car make a clear statement of your faith? Evangelize always—even on the road!

11. Make a "love note" holder for each family member and attach it to each bedroom door. Be "secret admirers" of each other and place anonymous notes in each holder. These can be notes of encouragement, inspirational quotations, or notes of apology. Perhaps time can be allowed at each evening meal to share any notes that are found that day.

12. As a family project, write your own religious allegory or parable. It can be as lengthy as Mother Loyola's *The King of the Golden City* or as short as the parable of the mustard seed. (See Matthew 13:31-32.)

13. Have a discussion regarding your family customs for the great feasts of Christmas and Easter. Are the seasons of Advent and Lent properly observed as preparation for these feasts? Examine the family customs currently in place regarding these celebrations. What other traditions can your family adopt to make these days more meaningful? A variety of books are available that offer numerous ideas on meaningful customs and practices. (See the list on pages 109-110 below for suggestions.)

14. Using a photo album or scrapbook, begin a family collection of holy cards. Most Catholic vendors sell these very reasonably. Older cards can be found in antique shops, and at rummage sales and thrift shops. They are sometimes found in old Bibles and prayer books. These make inexpensive gifts on birthdays and feast days, and as rewards for virtuous behavior.

15. Make a set of sacrifice beads to use as St. Therese did. Directions can be found in Ann Ball's book, *Catholic Traditions in Crafts* or online at http://thelittleways.com/how-to-make-sacrifice-beads. These are also frequently found in Catholic catalogs or online at . A similar option is to make a chaplet for your favorite saint or devotion. For example, put together on a ribbon or string, a medal of the Blessed Sacrament and thirty-three beads. On the medal, recite the following prayer: "As I cannot now receive Thee, my Jesus, in Holy Communion, come spiritually into my heart and make it Thine forever." On each bead recite the following: "Jesus in the Blessed Sacrament, have mercy on us!"

16. Plant a Mary garden or create an outside saint shrine—such as one to St. Francis. Research Mary gardens online at www.catholicculture.org/liturgicalyear/activities (under "Crafts."), www.fisheaters.com/marygardens.html, or www.mgardens.org, The book, *Mary's Flowers: Gardens, Legends & Meditations* by Vincenzina Krymow is available from St. Anthony Messenger Press.

17. Research several saints of the Eucharist. Begin with the following saints: Pope St. Pius X, St. Gerard, St. Gemma, St. Paschal, St. Tarcisius, or St. Maria Goretti. Why have

they been chosen as saints of the Eucharist? What other saints could be put into this category?

18. Create a portable flannel board for the Mass. Include figures for the Eucharistic ministers, lectors, cantors, deacons, and altar servers. Incorporate the different liturgical colors of the vestments. Use several symbolic vessels of the Mass as well as the altar itself. At home act out the Mass by manipulating the figures and the activities throughout the ceremony. If desired, such details as the kneelers, crucifix, lectionary, bread and wine, angels surrounding the altar, etc. can be included. Alternatively, organize on index cards pictures of the various vessels and figures of the Mass for younger children to take to church to provide a "matching" exercise to aid in following the Mass. For beginners, sort the cards in the order of their appearance in the Mass and as they get more adept, mix them before attending Mass.

19. Read another of Mother Mary Loyola's books, *First Communion and After*. Written by the author of *The King of the Golden City*, this book contains three parts: Our Lord's preparation for coming to us in Holy Communion (the life of Christ), our preparation for meeting Our Lord in Holy Communion, and "Thanks be to God for His unspeakable Gift." In this book, Mother Loyola instructs us to make a resolution after each chapter meditation; she provides step-by-step instructions for the Sacrament of Reconciliation and encourages children—through the use of stories and written illustrations—to prepare themselves to receive the Most Holy Sacrament.

20. Create an activity page based upon the next Sunday's reading for a younger sibling to take to Mass.

21. Conduct a family forgiveness ceremony by the family altar. Light candles to make it a solemn event. Prepare ahead by having each member write down at least one unloving act that they committed against another family member. Include a reading from the Bible and an examination of conscience from a penance preparation booklet or from a reflective reading of the Ten Commandments. Confess sins against each other aloud and conclude with an act of contrition—and hugs all around! Catholic Heritage Curricula has a book entitled *Family-Centered Examination of Conscience* that contains examens for parents, wives, husbands, and children as well as meditations, steps to reconciliation with God, and reflections on prayer, poverty, chastity, obedience, vocations, justice, and mercy. Conduct this ceremony at regular intervals throughout the year.

22. Begin a family collection of Catholic movies and/or read-aloud picture books. Search thrift stores such as St. Vincent de Paul for classic and Catholic family videos. Several Catholic vendors such as Ignatius Press (ignatius.com), Sacred Heart Books and Gifts (sacredheartbooksandgifts.com), Mother of Our Savior (moscompany.com), The Leaflet Missal Company (www.leafletonline.com), and Vision Video (catholicvideo.com) offer a wide selection. Purchase these as feast day gifts, Advent and Lenten gifts, or take turns each month choosing that month's movie purchase. You may also wish to begin a collection of Catholic picture books to read aloud. For starters, choose books from Catholic authors such as Tomie de Paola, Fr. Lawrence Lovasik, and Sr. Mary

Jean Dorcy; Catholic publishers such as Neumann Press and Catholic Book Publishing Company; and exceptional books such as *The Monk Who Grew Prayer* by Claire Brandenburg and *The Blackbird's Nest: St. Kevin of Ireland* by Jenny Schroedel. For a list of Catholic picture books, see the RACE for Heaven website at RACEforHeaven.com.

Community Projects

1. Tour some of the churches in your area—Catholic as well as other Christian churches. Try to visit the cathedral for your diocese as well as any missions in close proximity. View the inside structure as well as the outside architecture. Research and find out the history of the Christian faith in your diocese and your parish history in particular. Which is the oldest church in your area? Who were the early missionaries? When did they come and from where did they come? Are there any convents, monasteries, prayer chapels, retreat houses, or shrines within visiting distance? Spend as much time on this project as interest allows.

2. Interview your parish's first Communion teacher. Find out how long she/he has been teaching and what has changed in that period of time. What are the local customs for celebrating this sacrament? Interview your pastor—perhaps invite him to dinner and ask him to speak to your family about the sacraments of Holy Eucharist and Reconciliation. Perhaps he will be willing to share with you his memories of the sacraments as a priest and his own First Holy Communion.

3. Enjoy God in nature. Walk through the park, explore a cave, visit a zoo, swim in the ocean, listen to the wind, watch a waterfall, run through a meadow, stargaze, go to a planetarium (or a farm or aquarium), enjoy the sunset, stroll into a forest, or canoe a river. Read the creation story, the story of Noah's ark, or an appropriate Psalm—such as Psalm 65, Psalm 104, or Psalm 149. Each day remember to be grateful and aware of God's abiding Presence and the gifts of beauty He provides daily for us. Take photographs and/or compose poetry to capture the great outdoors.

4. Survey others regarding their impressions, thoughts and memories regarding the sacrament of Holy Communion. Contact grandparents, godparents, parents, siblings, nuns, priests, young children, an older man or woman from your parish, someone who doesn't receive Communion often, and/or someone from another country or culture to obtain their views. Ask your pastor for some names of elderly parishioners who are confined to a nursing home; interview them to discover their religious memories, and the customs and traditions of their generation. (This may result in a friendship of long standing.) Compile a range of opinions and ideas on this Most Holy Sacrament. Are there any common links in these remembrances?

5. Tour your parish church when Mass is not in progress. Do a careful examination of the interior of the church. What must be present to make a building a church? What fixtures are usually present in a Catholic Church? Examine the stained glass windows, the Stations of the Cross, the paschal candle, the statues and shrines, the confessional, the ceilings, the choir loft, the ambry, the prayer chapel, the holy water fonts, the sacristy, the tabernacle, the prayer garden, the baptismal font, the crucifix, the altar—and altar stones—and the pews. Some churches have booklets available that

explain different parts or furnishings of the church or the images in the stained glass windows. If your church does not have these, perhaps your family would like to provide the research to put together such a brochure. Try to sit in a different pew each time you attend Mass so younger children will be exposed to all parts of the church and the various activities and furnishings found there.

6. God has given us all special gifts and talents. Share your talents with others, and enjoy and appreciate the gifts He has given others. Teach someone else a craft or skill you have mastered; take a class to learn a new skill. Share a hobby with others by joining or starting a club. Visit a local art gallery or rock shop. The possibilities here are endless: chess, photography, bee-keeping, auto mechanics, needlework, or wood-working, to name but a few.

7. Read the excerpt "The Bread and Wine" from *The Mass Explained to Children* as contained on pages 113-114 below. Remember that the wine used for the consecration is pure grape wine; the recipe for the altar hosts is pure water and pure wheat baked in a waffle-like machine. Find out from your parish priest where the wine and hosts used in your parish are made. Although large corporations are producing many of the sacred elements used at Mass, some are still made in local monasteries and convents. If your parish uses materials locally produced, arrange to visit.

Long-Term Projects

1. Consider practicing any or all of the following Catholic celebrations and/or customs in your family:
   a) Obtain a Catholic calendar and begin to celebrate the feast days of saints special to family members—name day saints, patron saints, saints honored for special protection and devotion.
   b) Re-establish Sunday as a day dedicated to rest, family and individual prayer, and charitable works.
   c) Spread devotion to the Sacred Heart of Jesus and the Immaculate Heart of Mary by observing the First Fridays and First Saturdays of each month.
   d) Pray the Chaplet of Divine Mercy together daily (especially Friday) at three o'clock.
   e) Observe Friday as a day of penance in honor of Our Lord's sacrifice on that day. Abstain from meat or another food. The practice of penance on Fridays is still in effect for Catholics. See text paragraph 1438 in the *Catechism of the Catholic Church* for more information.
   f) Participate in special prayers each day and each month based upon the dedication of each week and month. For example, say a prayer to the holy angels or guardian angels on Tuesday, honor St. Joseph on Wednesday, or visit the cemetery in November to pray for the holy souls in Purgatory. If you are not able to attend daily Mass, obtain a missal and read the Mass readings for the day as a part of daily family prayers.
   g) Truly observe the penitential seasons of Advent and Lent.
   h) Begin to pray a family rosary each day or once a week.

i) Observe a family holy hour in front of the Blessed Sacrament each week. Each family member over the age of five or six can participate. Depending on the ages of the children, you may wish to begin with thirty minutes and work up to an hour. Consider the following activities: pray a five-decade rosary, walk the Stations of the Cross, read from Scripture, spend quiet moments listening to Jesus, write in a prayer journal, color in saint coloring books, make a novena of prayers (nine consecutive weeks) to specific saints, or sing hymns—if it would not disrupt others in church. Afterwards, take the children out for a treat and discuss each person's insights from the hour.

j) Become familiar with the Church's old observance of the seasons by reviving the penance of Rogation and Ember days. Use the Internet to research these penitential days if you are unfamiliar with them.

k) Celebrate St. Nicholas Day by leaving stockings out, light blessed candles on Candlemas, bury an Alleluia banner on Ash Wednesday, burn blessed palms when someone is traveling, read about the real St. Valentine—make sure to celebrate fully the feasts included in the Church's liturgical calendar.

In the pursuit of Catholic culture, any of the following books will be helpful. If you are just beginning to live a Catholic culture in your family, any of the first four are especially helpful.

i) *Catholic Customs and Traditions, A Popular Guide* by Greg Dues contains information on religious tradition, the Church year, the temporal cycle, the sanctoral cycle, sacramentals, and special days. (204 pages)

ii) *The Year and Our Children, Planning the Family Activities for Christian Feasts and Seasons* by Mary Reed Newland is a wonderful resource that covers all the major feasts and more unusual celebrations that bring home the lessons of each feast day and saint. (185 pages)

iii) *The How-To Book of Catholic Devotions, Step-by-Step Guidelines* by Mike and Regis J. Flaherty begins with the basics of how to pray and proceeds into Catholic prayers, a tradition of prayer, praying with Mary, penitential devotions, Eucharistic devotions, sacramentals and blessings, living the faith and where to learn more. (260 pages)

iv) *A Handbook of Catholic Sacraments* by Ann Ball is a very complete reference that provides information on topics such as blessings, relics, crucifixes and crosses, water, seasonal sacramentals, images, medals, scapulars and badges, chaplets, rosaries, and more. (205 pages)

v) *A Continual Feast, A Cookbook to Celebrate Family and Faith* by Evelyn Birge Vitz draws from the Catholic tradition over 275 recipes, ideas, and historical backgrounds for feast day celebrations, birthdays, baptisms, and Sunday dinners. (302 pages)

vi) *Customs and Traditions of the Catholic Family* by Neumann Press (originally titled *Your Home, A Church in Miniature*) covers many general family customs and provides a compilation of religious customs of various nationalities—German, Austrian, Mexican, Slovaks, Polish, Irish, Italian, Portuguese, French, and Russian Germans. (74 pages)

vii) *Religious Customs in the Family, The Radiation of the Liturgy into Catholic Homes* by Fr. Francis X. Weiser, S.J. contains general family customs to orient us toward heaven as well as seasonal customs such as Advent, Christmas, Holy Week, and special saints' feast days. (113 pages)

viii) *A Book of Feasts and Seasons* by Joanna Bogle attempts "to recapture the lost traditions surrounding our major feasts and festivals." With lengthier entries for many traditional feast days as well as many saints' feast days, this reference provides a short history of many of the saints as well as traditional methods of celebrating each day including traditional foods. (193 pages)

ix) *Catholic Traditions in Cooking, Catholic Traditions in Crafts, Catholic Traditions in the Garden,* and *Catholic Traditions in the Home and Classroom*—all written by Ann Ball, offer suggestions for celebrating the Church's liturgical seasons as well as feast days each month. (approximately 200 pages each)

2. Make some permanent changes regarding your family's attendance at Mass as well as the attitude and preparation for Mass. In order to prepare more adequately for this great celebration, arrive for Mass early. If you ride to Mass, consider using this time to prepare for receiving Him by reviewing the Scripture readings for the day or reading aloud from one of the Psalms. For those who enjoy music, consider singing hymns on the way to Mass or playing Catholic music on the tape or CD player. Observe a few moments of silent meditation. Find someone at Mass who looks lonely, does not fully participate, or that you know is going through a difficult time; "adopt" them for the week and offer special prayers and sacrifices for that person all week. Have your family remain after Mass for ten or fifteen minutes to offer a proper thanksgiving after Holy Communion. This can be a time of silent prayer; or if circumstances within the church allow, pray together the prayer to St. Michael or another prayer of the family's choosing. (See page 102 for a list of Psalms appropriate for the preparation for and thanksgiving of Holy Communion.)

3. Establish a "family night" for one convenient night of the week. Use this night to reestablish family bonds by playing board games, constructing a jigsaw puzzle, bowling, having a Catholic quiz night with small prizes, etc. Maybe a family music night would be enjoyed by your family; sing, dance, play any instruments you can find or make, or create your own family song. This could be family exercise night: go biking, hiking, running, play baseball, tennis, basketball, etc. Maybe Mom or Dad would like to coach one or more of the children in a sport. Occasionally, invite another family to join you for the evening's meal and activities.

4. Become familiar with the various ministries of your parish. Join and participate, or start your own ministry. Possible ministries include CCD teacher, RCIA teacher or sponsor, Bible study leader, Eucharistic minister, choir, cantor, lector, altar server, usher or greeter at Mass, youth group, Knights of Columbus, funeral assistance, pro-life

coordinator, natural family planning teacher or promoter, Blue Army (or other sodality), or outreach to the divorced, homebound or inactive parishioners. Consider any of the following activities: Adopt a family from a mission country to support. Start a sports or hobby club such as chess, volleyball, or basketball. Ask to help establish perpetual adoration in your parish. Organize a pilgrimage tour. Provide baby-sitting for parish functions. Begin a group to recite the rosary in church before Mass or at another specific time each day. Collect cans or labels. Establish a prayer chain for those in need. Set up a food pantry. Have a coffee social to welcome new parishioners. Begin a children's choir, Bible study or prayer group. Form an adult education class. Organize a mission. Help teach English and/or reading to adults. Provide a respite program for those caring for the elderly, sick or disabled. Plant a prayer garden. Help establish a parish lending library of religious books and/or videos. Provide medi-cal transportation to the sick, or transport those who would otherwise be unable to attend Mass. Run for parish council. Form a Catholic book club. Get involved!

5. Adopt a priest. Pray for this particular priest each day. Choose your parish priest, a priest you or your family may know from previous encounters, a priest in the media, a priest who administered a family sacrament—such as the parent's marriage, or a missionary priest. If he is a local priest, invite him to dinner. (This is a practice that has fallen out of fashion and should be revived!)

6. Research your family ancestry. Interview older relatives, and/or research using the Internet and a computer program designed for this purpose.

7. Get involved in a group worthy of assistance. "The poor you will always have with you." (Matthew 26:11) As a family, assist at a soup kitchen, become active in your local Habitat for Humanity, donate items—and time—to the St. Vincent de Paul Society, or visit the residents of a local nursing home, group home, adult day care center, or hospital. Become an active member of a pro-life group. Pray and make sacrifices each week for your special cause.

8. Continue to read aloud as a family. Read biographies of saints, classical literature, or the Bible. Establish a set time to do this; read every day at the same time. Or read one book, and then take break for a week or two before beginning another.

9. Establish a prayer time each day for all members of the family. This can be a period of ten or fifteen minutes when all can be present with God in the quiet of their rooms, or together in front of the family altar. A short reading can be read together or each can complete a reading of his/her own choice. Consider using a devotional book such as *The Imitation of Christ; My Daily Bread; Christian Prayer, The Liturgy of the Hours; My Daily Psalm Book; Magnificat;* or Our Sunday Visitor's *My Daily Visitor.*

Summary of Weekend Projects

Name of Project	Date Planned	Date Completed
Sacrament poster or banner		
Family coat of arms		
Consecration to the Sacred Heart		
Family patron saint		
Read *With Us Today*		
Rules for peaceful family living		
Study persecution of Christians today		
Family photo album or scrapbook		
Virtuous living		
Catholic home decorations		
Love notes		
Write family allegory or parable		
Examine family's religious customs		
Holy card collection		
Sacrifice beads or chaplet		
Mary garden		
Research Eucharistic saints		
Design flannel board for Mass		
Read *First Communion and After*		
Activity page for Mass		
Family forgiveness ceremony		
Catholic movie/book collection		
Tour area churches		
Interview teacher/pastor		
God in nature		
Survey memories of first Communion		
Inspect parish church		
Share talents/learn new skills		
Read "Bread and Wine"		
New Catholic family customs		
Refine Mass attitude and participation		
Family night celebration		
Church ministry involvement		
Adopt a priest		
Research ancestors		
Embrace a cause		
Read aloud regularly		
Institute family prayer time		

"The Bread and Wine"
from *The Mass Explained To Children* by Maria Montessori

The bread and wine of the Eucharistic table are the materials to be changed into the Body and Blood of Christ. After the consecration, what is present visibly is called the Species.

From a sense of devotion, Christians have always prepared these materials with special care, to mark their difference from what is used for the ordinary food of men. Their first tendency was to make them scrupulously from the very purest things. They have done this since the very earliest ages, even when they put on the altar the big, ordinary sort of loaf of bread that everyone used, but marked with a cross or with a fish, which was the symbol of Christ for the early Christians. The first Eucharistic breads were made of pure wheat, without any mixing, ground into flour, kneaded with pure water and then baked at the fire. Afterwards, instead of a loaf, wafers were used, but they were made in the same way and stamped with various sacred symbols. The Host used by the priest nowadays is large and ornamented with such symbols; while the hosts, or particles (little portions), given to the faithful in Holy Communion, are much smaller and often have nothing stamped on them.

Then the wine is made of pure grape-juice, without any mixture. Only, when the pure wine is in the Chalice, the priest adds a little water. This action recalls an incident in the Passion, when the soldier pierced the side of Christ and blood and water issued.

That is why such ordinary things as the wheat and the grape have such tremendous importance for us Christians. They become a mysterious food, which only we can understand. Just as our soul lives in the world by means of the flesh of our bodies, so God remains among us under the Species which come from the wheat and the grape. After the consecration the *latens deitas*, the Hidden Godhead, lies under those humble appearances.

The cultivation of the plants destined for such noble use inspires Christians with great devotion; even the clods of earth which feed these plants have something sacred for us which sets them apart. The fields of wheat and the vines that are to give the bread and wine for the Eucharist cannot be confused with the vast fields of corn and the rich vineyards which man cultivates for himself in the sweat of his brow.

The former are almost "particles" of earth, small plots, because very little corn and only a very small vine are sufficient to provide the materials for the Eucharist.

This is the reason why the plan was formed in Italy some years ago of turning over to the children the cultivation of such plots. It had already been done in a school in Barcelona. Two fields were set apart for the purpose, side by side, one for the wheat and the other for the vine. These fields were surrounded with flowering plants which would give flowers in every season, especially an abundance of roses.

The harvesting of the wheat and the vintage of the wine were then made great country festivals, carried out with the most beautiful ceremonies.

The idea that children are the most suitable for cultivating the Eucharistic fields, and for taking part in the making of the hosts and the wine, is only the latest of many such devout ideas which Christians have had from the very earliest times.

At one time it was the most illustrious and powerful personages in the kingdom, such as queens and princes, who reserved this honor for themselves; one old writer says: ". . . I saw with my own eyes Candida, the wife of Trajan, General-in-Command of the armies of Valerius, spend the whole night in grinding the wheat and making with her own hands the bread of oblation. . . ."

The holy Queen Radegonde used to make the Eucharistic bread and bake it during Lent.

Towards the end of the ninth century, a cardinal recommended deacons, chosen to make the altar-breads, to vest themselves in their blessed habits for this work and to sing psalms while they were doing it.

It is said that in some parts of France it used to be the custom to choose the wheat grain by grain; and the very holiest person in the district was chosen to take it to the mill, dressed in white, as in a solemn ceremony.

Even a reverence for the sod of earth is related in ancient history. People used to leave as heritage little plots of ground that they loved, dedicating them to the cultivation of the wheat that would supply "the pure, holy and stainless Host."

It is faith that makes people do these things: those who are imbued with faith show a great delicacy of love in all their actions.

Communion with the Saints, A Family Preparation Program for First Communion and Beyond in the Spirit of St. Therese

Answer Key

The Little Flower, The Story of St. Therese of the Child Jesus

Chapter 1—In Which Therese Is Born and Thrives

1. Some people thought that the marriage between Therese's parents was a mistake as they felt both were too holy to live in the world. A few people felt that Therese's parents should live their lives not as married people in the world but as religious people within a monastery.
2. Mr. and Mrs. Martin gave all of their children—even the boys—the first name of Marie, which is French for "Mary." In this way, each child was consecrated to the Blessed Virgin. It was important for the Martins to have a boy as they wished to give a son to the priesthood to serve God.
3. Therese was born on Thursday, January 2, 1873—the youngest child of Louis and Zelie Martin. Her full name was Marie Frances Therese Martin.
4. Therese was sent to live in the country with a nurse, as her mother's ongoing battle with breast cancer prevented her from breastfeeding Therese. In addition, Therese could receive plenty of fresh air and sunshine.

Chapter 2—In Which Therese Begins to Love Jesus

1. Therese's father called Therese his "Little Queen."
2. Mr. Martin made his living as a watchmaker and jeweler; he quit this business near the end of 1870 in order to assist Mrs. Martin in her business as a "Maker of Point d'Alencon"—a craftswoman of fine Alencon lace. (See pages 34-36 of *The Story of a Family, The Home of St. Thérèse of Lisieux* by Fr. Stéphane-Joseph Piat, O.F.M. for more details or use an encyclopedia for pictures; see "lace.")
3. At the age of three, Therese decided to become a nun; this was the same time that her older sister Pauline decided to pursue a religious vocation at Carmel.

Chapter 3—In Which Therese Loses Her Mother and Continues to Grow in the Good God's Grace

1. The Martin's new home in Lisieux was called Les Buissonnets, which is translated into English as "a wooded estate" or The Elms.
2. Mr. Martin explains that the Carmelite nuns are hidden from the world (or "cloistered") so that they can give all their time to loving God and bringing others to love Him.
3. The priest's blessing brought no visible effect to Therese's rosary beads, but Pauline explained that the prayers offered with the rosary would be more pleasing to God.

Chapter 4—In Which Therese Attends School and Becomes Very Ill

1. Although her sister Pauline (or her "little mother" as Therese called her), had taught Therese at home, she was almost nine before she attended school outside her home. It was then that she began her formal studies at the Benedictine convent as a day student.

2. Upon her admission to Carmel, Pauline received the name of "Sr. Agnes of Jesus." Should Therese later be admitted, as was her current wish, she would be given the name of "Sr. Therese of the Child Jesus."

3. Immediately before Therese's cure from her mysterious illness, she felt the devil battling for her soul. She tried to run from him but could not. Her sisters prayed desperately for her, especially Marie who implored our mother Mary to spare Therese's life. Suddenly, Therese felt at peace; the statue of the Blessed Virgin that was in the room became alive for her and smiled. Therese was cured.

Chapter 5—In Which Therese Receives Her First Communion and Confirmation, and Her Prayers for Peace Are Answered

1. Therese received her first Holy Communion on May 8, 1883, at the age of eleven. She had begun her preparation four years earlier when Pauline had prepared Celine for first Holy Communion. In addition to Therese's instruction at the Benedictine convent, Marie also assisted each evening in her preparation. Pauline, now Sr. Agnes, wrote numerous letters to Therese from the convent to assist in preparing Therese for Holy Communion; Pauline also composed a little notebook of prayers and devotions for Therese entitled, Two Months and Nine Days of Preparation for My First Communion. Therese attended a retreat at the convent for the entire week before the sacrament was to be given. In addition, Therese began to mediate for at least fifteen minutes each day. Therese made these resolutions after receiving her first Holy Communion: I will never give way to discouragement. I will say the *Memorare* every day. I will try to humble my pride. (Note that while Therese made her first confession at the age of six, she did not receive her first Holy Communion until five years later.)

2. Therese received the Sacrament of Confirmation five weeks after her first Holy Communion. She prayed for the gift of fortitude as she felt the joy of her first Communion slipping away.

3. The second miracle Therese felt was performed for her was in answer to her prayer for peace and a loss of her extreme self-consciousness. She was very sensitive and cried easily. She prayed that God would help her overcome this—to "grow up." On Christmas morning 1886, she felt her prayers were answered as she truly began to realize that all of God's children have been given a portion of the strength of the Child Jesus.

Chapter 6—In Which Therese's Soul Thirsts for Sinners and Grows in Grace

1. When a picture of the Crucifixion slipped out of Therese's prayer book showing one of the Savior's pierced hands, Therese was struck with an intense longing to suffer for the conversion of sinners. This occurred a short time after her conversion experience around Christmas 1886.
2. Therese joined the Carmelites as opposed to a missionary order as she felt called to sacrifice for sinners by leading a life of prayer and penance.
3. Therese delayed speaking to her father for several weeks about her decision to enter Carmel as she felt he had been very generous already in giving up three other daughters to the cloistered life of a nun.
4. Many people were opposed to Therese entering Carmel at the age of fourteen or fifteen including her Uncle Isidore, her sister Marie, and Canon Delatroette (the priest in charge of the affairs of the Carmelite community of Lisieux).

Chapter 7—In Which Therese Speaks to the Holy Father Regarding Entrance to Carmel

1. In Paris at the church of Our Lady of Victories, Therese had this question answered, "Had Our Lady really smiled on Therese and cured her when she was ten years old"? Our Lady let her know that she had indeed restored Therese to good health through the smile on the image of Our Lady's statue; it was not mere imagination.
2. At the Coliseum, Therese asked God to let her be a martyr, "Dear Lord, please let me be a martyr, too!" (page 67)
3. Pope Leo XIII's reaction to Therese's request to enter Carmel at the age of fifteen was to tell her to do whatever the superiors in charge decided. He assured her that if it be God's will for her to enter, then she would.

Chapter 8—In Which Therese Begins Her Life as a Carmelite Nun

1. Therese and her family took a pilgrimage to Rome that lasted about a month.
2. Mother Gonzago wanted to wait until the difficult sacrifices and penances the Carmelites undertook during the season of Lent were completed before admitting Therese to Carmel.
3. Therese wished to enter Carmel to escape the trials and temptations of life in the world. However, her main goal was to save souls by giving her life, in union with Jesus, for the redemption of sinners. She felt she should not seek any pleasure, even the most innocent, as these sacrifices were pleasing to God.
4. For exercise at Carmel, Therese was given the task of weeding the garden.

Chapter 9—In Which Therese Continues to Lead a Life of Sacrifice for the Salvation of Sinners

1. Therese received the habit of the Carmelite order, becoming a novice, on January 10, 1889. She was sixteen years old.
2. Therese's special charge in the chapel was the shrine of the Child Jesus—the statue of the Infant Jesus.

3. Canon Delatroette delayed Therese's Profession of Solemn Vows for eight months. A new date set was September 8, 1890, several months before her eighteenth birthday.

Chapter 10—In Which Therese Professes Her Vows and Lives Her Vocation
1. The night before her Profession Day, the devil put an anxious fear in her mind, causing her to doubt her vocation as a professed religious at Carmel.
2. One thought concerning her vocation that Therese pondered after her father's death was the fact that she had come to Carmel to save souls—and especially to pray for priests. The second thought was her preference for sacrifice over all ecstasies—she preferred to serve God and imitate Him rather than to have her senses full of Him.
3. Because of the influenza epidemic in 1891, Therese was given the privilege of receiving the Eucharist daily.

Chapter 11—In Which Therese Begins to Write Her Autobiography
1. As Assistant Novice Mistress, Therese instructed the novices under her care in the Little Way to Heaven as developed by Therese herself.
2. Therese's Profession Day was on September 8, 1990. Leonie was accepted into the Visitation order in Caen several months after Therese began her work with the novices in February of 1893. Therefore, it was almost three years before God granted this petition of Therese's. (Note that Leonie entered the Visitation convent in Caen on June 24, 1893. She stayed at the Visitation convent until 1895; however, she returned in 1899 and stayed as a Visitandine until her death in 1941.)
3. Celine had misgivings about entering Carmel as she feared she would not be able to follow the rigorous Rule. There were also difficulties in obtaining permission for her entrance as three of her sisters were already professed nuns there.
4. In December 1894, Therese's sister Marie suggested to Pauline, then Mother Prioress, that Therese write down her childhood memories. Marie thought that Therese could show what wonderful parents the Martins had and provide spiritual insight that would be helpful to others.
5. Therese herself entitled her autobiography, *The Story of the Springtime of a Little White Flower*. She was remembering the white lily her father had picked and given her the night she spoke to him of her vocation and intention to enter Carmel. "Springtime" denotes her youth.

Chapter 12—In Which Therese Continues to Guide Souls along the Path of Spiritual Childhood
1. Therese, who had already abandoned her will to God and was following her Little Way of childlike trust, offered herself as a victim soul of His love.
2. The only fear Therese had was that of keeping her own will. She wanted God to take it; she would do whatever God decided for her.
3. Three important events in Therese's life that took place in 1895 include the following: a) the beginning the writing of her autobiography b) the profession of her Act of Love and Oblation and c) the entrance of her cousin, Marie Guerin, into Carmel.

4. Therese was delighted to correspond with the priestly missionaries as she herself desired to become a priest and serve the Foreign Missions. The priesthood was close to her heart, and she was willing to suffer in any way to bring the Word of God to pagan lands. This was her way of bringing the Holy Faith to pagan lands; she could be a channel of grace for the labors of priests.

Chapter 13—In Which Therese Contracts Tuberculosis and Dreams of Being Called to Heaven Soon

1. Therese feels she has only a few months—a year or two at the most—yet to live. (Therese receives this premonition in the spring of 1896 and dies in September of 1897—a year and a half later.)
2. As Marie perceives that Therese may have little time left to live, she asks Therese to write about her spirituality—just as she wrote about her childhood memories.
3. Therese claims that one of her greatest sufferings while at Carmel was the coldness of her cell.

Chapter 14—In Which Therese and Her Sisters Prepare for Therese's Death

1. Therese stated, "People cannot be free or happy until they have renounced all claims to freedom and happiness. Only when they have seen themselves as little children, depending on God's mercy for the very air they breathe, can they find peace." (page 148)
2. When she placed in the Infirmary the statue of the Blessed Virgin who had once smiled upon Therese, Marie hoped for a similar miracle—a cure for Therese.
3. Therese wished to lead souls by the way of spiritual childhood, the way of confidence and self-surrender. She would like to show souls the Little Way that succeeded so perfectly with her. (page 150)
4. Three predictions Therese made before her death include a) that there would be a shower of roses when she died b) that she would not only look down on us from Heaven, but come down and c) that some day everyone is going to love her.

Chapter 15—In Which Therese Continues Doing Good upon Earth

1. Therese wished to imitate Christ by undergoing a death like His—one of agonizing sufferings.
2. Therese expected others to see God in a new light after reading her book. They would discover that He was not only their Judge but also their Father, and thousands of people would forget their fear of Him. They would joyfully set about achieving holiness by becoming little children.
3. Celine and Therese took the turtledove that appeared on the windowsill near the bed of Therese bed as a sign of Therese's impending death. They recalled the words of Scripture in which the Lord calls his beloved. (Song of Songs 2:10-14, or Canticle of Canticles 2:10-14 in Douay-Rheims translation)

The Children of Fatima and Our Lady's Message to the World

Chapter 1—In Which the Angel of Peace Teaches the Shepherd Children to Pray

1. Three children were present during the appearances of the angel: six-year-old Jacinta Marto; her brother Francisco, who was eight; and their cousin Lucia dos Santos, aged nine.

2. As they watched their parents' sheep each day, the children amused themselves by talking, playing in a nearby cave, playing the "echo game", building houses out of stones, or playing in the fields with the sheep. They always made time for the rosary after lunch—a shortened version of it at least.

3. Francisco did not like reciting the rosary or going to church; he felt such things were only for women and girls.

4. Between the spring and fall of 1916, the angel appeared to the children three times, teaching them two prayers to recite and asking them to offer prayers and sacrifices to the Most High. In the spring of 1916, the angel appeared identifying himself as the "Angel of Peace"; he taught them a prayer to be prayed with their foreheads touching the ground. In mid-summer, he again appeared, identifying himself as the "Angel of Portugal"—its Angel Guardian. He asked them to pray continually and instructed them to offer sacrifices as reparation to God. In the fall of 1916, the angel again appeared to the three shepherd children to teach them another prayer to recite. At this time, he also gave them Holy Communion.

Discussion Topics

St. Faustina also reports of receiving Holy Communion from an angel in April of 1938 while she was confined to a sanatorium: "Jesus said to me, Be at peace; I am with you. Tired, I fell asleep. In the evening, the sister (Sr. David) who was to look after me came and said, 'Tomorrow you will not receive the Lord Jesus, Sister, because you are very tired; later on, we shall see.' This hurt me very much, but I said with great calmness, 'Very well,' and, resigning myself totally to the will of the Lord, I tried to sleep. In the morning, I made my meditation and prepared for Holy Communion, even though I was not to receive the Lord Jesus. When my love and desire had reached a high degree, I saw at the bedside a Seraph, who gave me Holy Communion saying these words: 'Behold the Lord of Angels.' When I received the Lord, my spirit was drowned in the love of God and in amazement. This was repeated for thirteen days, although I was never sure he would bring me Holy Communion the next day. Yet, I put my trust completely in the goodness of God, but did not even dare to think that I would receive Holy Communion in this way on the following day.

"The Seraph was surrounded by a great light, the divinity and love of God being reflected in him. He wore a golden robe and, over it, a transparent surplice and a transparent stole. The chalice was crystal, covered with a transparent veil. As soon as he gave me the Lord, he disappeared.

"Once, when a certain doubt rose within me shortly before Holy Communion, the Seraph with the Lord Jesus stood before me again. I asked the Lord Jesus, and not receiving an answer, I said to the Seraph, 'Could you perhaps hear my confession?' And he answered me, 'No spirit in heaven has that power.' And at that moment, the Sacred Host rested on my lips." (Diary, 1676-77)

Chapter 2—In Which Our Lady Visits the Shepherd Children

1. Our Lady first appeared to the shepherd children on May 13, 1917, slightly more than a year after the angel's first visit.
2. While Lucia and Jacinta both heard and saw our Lady, only Lucia spoke with her; Francisco was able to see our Lady but could not hear the words she spoke.
3. The children agreed to keep the visit of the lady a secret because they did not feel anyone would believe them. "Alas for the cherished secret!" (page 16)

Chapter 3—In Which Our Lady Gives the Children Another Prayer and Promises to Take Jacinta and Francisco to Heaven Soon

1. Both mothers were very angry, as they did not believe the children. They took the children to the parish priest, as they were unable to get the children to admit that they were telling a lie. The priest, Father Ferreira, felt that the children had imagined the vision as he did not believe they would deliberately lie.
2. Father Ferreira advised the children's mothers not to punish them anymore.
3. Around seventy people gathered in the sheep pasture on June 13, 1917, in anticipation of our Lady's visit to the children. Our Lady asked the children to continue to pray and make sacrifices for sinners and taught them a prayer to add to the rosary after each Glory Be. She told Lucia that she wanted her to learn to read as she would stay for some time on earth, while she would take Jacinta and Francisco to heaven with her soon.

Chapter 4—In Which Our Lady Continues the Message of Her Second Visit

1. When our Lady stretched out her hands toward the children, rays of light extended from the Lady's hands to their hearts, bringing a love and warmth they had never known before.
2. Our Lady requested the devotion of the Five First Saturdays to make her Heart known and loved by others. Attached to this devotion is Mary's promise to assist, at the hour of death, with all graces necessary for that soul to obtain salvation.
3. Some of the onlookers at the second visit began to believe that the lady had actually been at the holm-oak as they had observed the tree prior to the visit; they noticed after the lady's visit that the top branches of the tree had been bent to the east.

Chapter 5—In Which the Children Receive Three Secrets from Our Lady and Experience a Vision of Hell

1. Approximately five thousand people attended the expected third visit of our Lady to the children of Fatima on July 13, 1917. This is compared with seventy people who had attended in June.

2. The first secret of this message was the vision of hell; the second secret involved devotion to the Blessed Virgin and the consecration of Russia. (Lucia revealed both of these visions in 1927; the third secret, regarding the vision of the bishop/pope, was not revealed until May 13, 2000.)

3. Lucia's life at home changed considerably in the months following the first visit of our Lady. Her mother, concerned about the gossip regarding Lucia and the entire dos Santos family, had begun to beat and scold Lucia hoping she would confess her "lie." Lucia's sisters and brother felt she was bringing disgrace upon the family; people would whisper and point as they walked by giving them no peace. Lucia herself was questioned at all times and places by many people who wanted to speak with her regarding the visits and messages.

Chapter 6—In Which the Mayor Prevents the Children from Meeting with Our Lady

1. The mayor of Ourem was upset about the events at Fatima as he did not believe in God and did not understand the events taking place. In addition, he was responsible for keeping peace in the territory surrounding Fatima; he felt the apparitions might cause a disturbance.

2. Lucia's reaction to the questions of the mayor was calm, respectful, and firm; she was not intimidated and refused to back down regarding the visions of the lady.

3. As Lucia would not promise not to go to the Cova on August 13th, the mayor developed a scheme to prevent the children from going. He decided to kidnap them.

Chapter 7—In Which the Faith and Spiritual Courage of the Children Are Tested

1. The other prisoners were amazed at the courage of Lucia, Jacinta, and Francisco. They acted respectfully toward them—some in fact even joined in the recitation of the rosary with them.

2. On the fifth day of the children's imprisonment, the mayor's patience with the children ran out. He decided to take drastic measures and told the children that unless they told the "truth" about the Lady, he would boil them alive in oil.

3. When she thought that Jacinta and Francisco had been killed, Lucia stretched out her arms toward heaven and begged our Lady to give her the strength to die as bravely as Jacinta and Francisco did.

Chapter 8—In Which the Events of August 13th Are Told, and Our Lady Makes Her August Visit

1. The crowd who gathered for the lady's visit on August 13th got a miracle: they heard a clap of thunder, then saw a flash of lightning. The sun began to pale, and a glowing cloud settled about the little holm-oak and hid it from view. Many more people came to believe that the events of Fatima were supernatural.

2. On August 19th while the children were shepherding their sheep near the village of Valinhos, our Lady appeared to the children. The lady was very displeased with the mayor of Ourem and stated that all Portugal will share in the punishment for his cruelty—the miracle of October 1917 will be much less impressive. She told Lucia

what to do with the gifts left by the holm-oak; she again encouraged the children to recite the rosary each day and to continue to make many sacrifices for sinners.

3. Our Lady told Lucia to use some of the gifts to buy stretchers to be used in processions in honor of our Lady; the rest were to be used to begin the erection of a chapel in honor of Our Lady of the Rosary.

Chapter 9—In Which Our Lady Gives Her Fifth Message to the Children of Fatima

1. Thirty thousand people were expected for the September apparition, compared to the fifteen thousand who were present for the August vision.

2. Several signs signaled the approach of the lady including a clap of thunder, a bolt of lightning, the dimming of the sun, and the appearance of a small, shining cloud over the holm-oak.

3. Not all the people present for the fifth visit of our Lady believed the apparitions of Fatima were supernatural in nature. Many continued to believe it was a trick performed for attention or money.

Chapter 10—In Which the Great Miracle of the Sun Occurs

1. At least sixty thousand people were expected to attend the promised miracle that was to occur on October 13, 1917. The children were confident that the lady would come and the miracle would occur as promised. However, Lucia's mother was worried that all would not go well, and her family would be disgraced.

2. The mission of the messages given by our Lady of Fatima was to instill in the hearts of not only the three children but also in the hearts of all Catholics a knowledge of the great power of the rosary as well as a willingness to recite this prayer daily.

3. While Jacinta and Francisco had shared Lucia's vision of the Holy Family, Lucia herself had also enjoyed a vision of our Lord accompanied by His mother as our Lady of Sorrows. Then our Lady had appeared to Lucia as Our Lady of Mount Carmel.

Chapter 11—In Which the Children Begin to Live according to the Instructions of Our Lady

1. The miracle of the sun was seen not only in the Cova da Iria but also throughout all of Portugal.

2. In Lucia's family, there were four girls and one boy: Therese, Gloria, Caroline, Lucia, and Manuel.

3. In their description of the vision of hell, the children describe "billions and billions" of damned souls.

Chapter 12—In Which the Children Attend School, and Francisco Receives His First Holy Communion

1. Despite the staring and whispering of the other children, the three children wanted to stay in school as it gave them the opportunity to study their catechism and to visit Jesus in the Blessed Sacrament.

2. The Blessed Virgin appeared again to Jacinta and Francisco near the end of October 1918 while they were at home alone. She told them that soon she would take Francisco to heaven but that Jacinta would stay and suffer a while longer.
3. Francisco was troubled by the fact that he had not yet received his First Holy Communion, upon which he had his heart set on receiving before his death.

Chapter 13—In Which Jacinta's Suffering Increases
1. Francisco Martos died of influenza on April 4, 1919.
2. Our Lord has entrusted the peace of the world to the Immaculate Heart of Mary.

Chapter 14—In Which We Learn of Jacinta's Love for Sinners as She Continues to Suffer and Make Sacrifices
1. Jacinta went to Ourem at the request of her parents who wished her to undergo treatments for the painful abscess in her side; after two months of regular medical treatment, which was unsuccessful, she was sent home in August of 1919.
2. Jacinta and her mother went to Lisbon in January 1920 so that a specialist could examine Jacinta. In Lisbon she stayed for two weeks at an orphanage before being admitted to the hospital for her surgery, which she had on February 10th.
3. The two privileges Jacinta received at the orphanage that she described as "heaven on earth" were her visits to the Blessed Sacrament and her frequent reception of Holy Communion.
4. Jacinta's last great sacrifice came on the evening before her death when a visiting priest heard her confession but refused to give her Holy Communion as he felt she was not in danger of death.

Chapter 15—In Which Lucia Leaves Fatima
1. After a year a suffering, Jacinta died on February 20, 1920. She was buried in Baron d'Alvayazer's family vault at Ourem. (However, in 1935, her body was moved to the Fatima cemetery next to Francisco.)
2. In addition to the inability to visit the grave of Jacinta, Lucia also suffered when the atheistic government of Portugal tried to close the Cova da Iria as a place of devotion.
3. On June 17, 1921, Lucia, at the request of the bishop, went to the convent boarding school of the Sisters of St. Dorothy at Vilar. The bishop felt that Lucia needed a better school than the one at Fatima as well as some privacy from the constant flow of pilgrims who wanted to see her.
4. The bishop also insisted that Lucia take a new name so no one at the convent would know that she was Lucia, the visionary, to whom the Blessed Virgin had appeared. Her new name was to be Maria das Dores.

(Lucia took her perpetual vows as a sister of Saint Dorothy on October 3, 1934. Due to her need for solitude and seclusion, she desired to become a Discalced Carmelite. She received permission from Pope Pius XII to do so and joined the Carmelite order on March 25, 1948. The Blessed Virgin reportedly appeared to her several times in her adult life. After a long illness, Sr. Mary Lucia of the Immaculate Heart died on February 13, 2005, at her Carmelite convent in Coimbra, Portugal, at the age of 97.)

The Patron Saint of First Communicants, The Story of Blessed Imelda

Chapter 1—In Which Imelda Is Born

1. The story of Blessed Imelda takes place in Bologna, a city in northern Italy, beginning in the year of her birth, 1322.
2. Peter felt that John's son returned home "only because of prayer." (page 2)
3. Peter starts out to see Donna Castora to thank her for her prayers for Phillip and tell her that Phillip has come back. However, he does not get to tell her due to the excitement of the birth of Donna's child.
4. The castle bells were ringing to celebrate the birth of the Lambertini's daughter. Peter stated that, according to common custom, the bells were usually only rung if the new child was a boy.

Chapter 2—In Which Donna Castora Dreams of St. Dominic

1. The Lambertini's celebrated the birth of their daughter by providing free food and wine to all.
2. Donna Castora dreamed that she had met St. Dominic and that he had given her a special smile and blessing. She felt that great things were in store for Imelda.
3. Donna Castora's brother, the archbishop, advised her that some dreams are sent for a special purpose but that she must not read too much into the dream.

Chapter 3—In Which Imelda Longs for Our Lord

1. Some of the gifts that God had bestowed upon Imelda included physical beauty, a quick mind, and an unselfish spirit. She loved to make others happy.
2. For her fifth birthday, Imelda wished to receive our Lord in Holy Communion "just like grownup people do." (page 30) Her parents were unable to grant this wish as Church regulations at that time required that a child be fourteen years old to receive Holy Communion. (This rule was changed to the age of seven by Pope Pius X in 1910.)
3. Of all the gifts she received, Imelda's favorite was the pearl rosary given to Imelda by her mother.

Chapter 4—In Which Imelda Shares Her Knowledge of the Dominican Order

1. Tarcisius and St. Agnes were Imelda's imaginary companions. She often asked them to help her love God as He wishes to be loved.
2. By the time she was nine, Imelda's attitude toward receiving Holy Communion was one of patient resignation. She felt God had a reason for making her wait to receive Him, and she tried to be satisfied in waiting as He wished.
3. Beatrice was uneasy over Imelda's account of the Dominican saints as she felt such deep thoughts were far beyond Imelda's years.
4. Imelda prayed daily that God would give Peter back his sight.
5. During her visit to the Sisters of St. Agnes Convent, Imelda wished that she had known Blessed Diana and that she could love our Lord as the sisters did.

Chapter 5—In Which Imelda Joins the Convent of St. Mary Magdalen

1. Imelda entered the Dominican convent of St. Mary Magdalen in Bologna, Italy, at age nine.
2. As she gave herself to God's service and received the Dominican habit, Imelda asked for "God's mercy and yours" [the superior's]. (page 54)
3. Some of the virtues Imelda was expected to acquire as a novice included obedience and humility. She needed to be willing to act as a servant to others and to bear all trials.
4. In the convent Imelda was assigned charge of the poor who came to the monastery for food.

Chapter 6—In Which Our Lord Comes to Imelda in an Unexpected Way

1. The tradition of the Church (Church rule) during the fourteenth century was that children must be fourteen years of age to receive Holy Communion.
2. Imelda states that neither the angels nor saints in heaven can receive Holy Communion; but anyone who has the True Faith and keeps the Commandments (is in the state of grace) may receive our Lord in the Eucharist.
3. Several of the nuns believed that Imelda was crying as the spring weather was causing her to be homesick. The real reason for her tears, however, was that she was disappointed about the continued delay in receiving our Lord in Holy Communion.
4. This chapter's miracle is the presence of a consecrated Host floating above Imelda's head. This Host, accompanied by a strange light and a marvelous fragrance of flowers, had moved from above the altar, through the cloister grating, and across the chapel to rest above Imelda's head.

Chapter 7—In Which Imelda's Dream Comes True

1. The nuns remained in humble thanksgiving for more than an hour after witnessing the miracle of the floating Host.
2. After leaving Imelda in the chapel, the Prioress described Holy Communion as the greatest privilege in the world—a proof, if one were needed, of God's immense love for all mankind.
3. Due to the intercession of Imelda, her parents came to the convent after her death, dry-eyed and calm. While grieving, they accepted God's will with eagerness and trust, without question or complaint.
4. The first miracle attributed to the intercession of Imelda after her death was the return of vision to the blind basket-maker, Peter.

The King of the Golden City, An Allegory for Children

Parallel Figures Chart

(There are many different "correct answers" for any of the following parallel figures. The answers below represent possible meanings. Do not be limited to them. Accept any parallel meaning that can be supported.)

Chapter 1—The Meeting in the Wood
THE KING—Jesus
THE GOLDEN CITY—our heavenly home
THE COUNTRY OF THE TRAVELERS (LAND OF EXILE)—earth
THE REBEL LORD MALIGNUS—Satan, the devil
THE HAPPY ONES—the saints in heaven
THE MAID—each of us
THE MAID'S HUT—the maid's body, her heart
THE WILDFLOWERS—virtues practiced and sacrifices made
THE KING'S SIMPLE ROBE OF WHITE—Jesus' appearance in the Host
THE QUARTER OF AN HOUR SPENT WITHIN THE HUT TOGETHER—the time of His physical presence with each of us after receiving Him in Holy Communion, our time of thanksgiving after Communion
THE PATH TO THE HUT—our preparation for Holy Communion
THE WOUNDS OF THE KING—his sufferings and wounds obtained on the cross for us
THE UNCLEAN HUT—our soul when it is not adequately prepared to receive Him in Communion
NO FIT SPOT TO LAY THEM (THE KING'S GIFTS) DOWN—a soul not adequately prepared to receive Him or a soul in the state of sin

Chapter 2—The Little Maid Finds She Must Help in Her Own Training
LIEUTENANTS—the pope and other bishops
PRINCE OF THE COURT (PRINCE GUARDIAN)—guardian angel
TEACHERS—priests, CCD teachers, parents, Holy Scripture, the Church, our guardian angel

Chapter 3—The King's Laws
SIGNS—commandments, laws of the Church, precepts of Holy Scripture and the sacraments
THE STRAIGHT ROAD—the way of the Cross, following Jesus, the way of grace

Chapter 4—The King's Household
A LARGE HOUSE—the Catholic Church and the treasury of the Church
THE SCHOOL—the teachings and doctrines of the Church, the catechism, Holy Scripture
THE GYMNASIUM—the family
THE ARMORY—the Sacrament of Confirmation
THE HOSPITAL OR INFIRMARY—the sacraments of Reconciliation and Anointing of the Sick

THE BANQUET HALL—the Sacrament of the Eucharist

THE ROYAL AUDIENCE CHAMBER—the church where Mass is held and the tabernacle resides

Chapter 5—A Troublesome Partner

SELF—our self-love, our free will, our tendency toward sin, our conscience, temptations of the flesh

LAMP OF "PEACE"—God's gift of grace, His life in us, the theological virtues of faith, hope and love

Chapter 6—The King's Table

DAILY BANQUET—the great gift of daily reception of our Lord in Holy Communion

THE WHITE ROBE—our soul when in the state of grace

ANTE-CHAMBER—confessional

SMALL STAINS ON THE WHITE ROBE—venial sins

JEWELS WITH WHICH THE KING ADORNED THE WHITE ROBE—grace

Chapter 7—Dilecta Asks for a Change

BRIDGET—a person who has stayed true to Jesus despite adversity and temptation; a virtuous person willing to carry the cross of suffering

Chapter 8—The King's Armory

SOLDIERS OF THE ROYAL ARMY—confirmed members of the Catholic Church

ENROLLED IN MY ARMY—confirmed in the Church, a soldier of Christ

JOLLY ONES OR TRIFLERS—those not concerned about life everlasting, non-Christians or non-practicing Christians

Chapter 9—The King's Infirmary

WOUNDED SOLDIERS—those with unconfessed sins on their souls

SULLIED WHITE ROBE—the robe of those with unpardoned sins on their souls

Chapter 10—The Little Maid in an Idle Mood

MASTER OF HIS OWN HOUSE—master of his own soul, one who has a well-formed conscience

SOFT KNOCK AT THE DOOR—the subtle tempting of the devil, temptation, near occasion of sin

Chapter 11—The Broad Road

THE FAIR—the world where both Christians and non-Christians live together, the pleasure of the world where it is necessary to discern which activities and amusements are appropriate for a Christian

THE PLAY—pleasures that are not Christian

DAISY—peer pressure

THE BROAD ROAD—time-wasting pleasures that do not bring us closer to Jesus and are not pleasing to Him; temptations of the world

Chapter 12—The Fair

BAD SWEETS SPRINKLED WITH SUGAR—activities, thoughts, or actions that appear on the outside, without much thought or observation, to be harmless that are in fact not

POISONOUS POWDERS—evil thoughts, sacrilegious ideas, unchaste thoughts

DARK VALLEY—God's seat of Justice where the punishments of the dead are given, first step toward Purgatory or hell

Chapter 13—The Little Maid Learns Some Lessons

FOOT SLIPPED IN CROSSING THE ROAD—venial sin

MOTOR (CAR) CAME AND DROVE OVER YOU—mortal sin

Chapter 14—What the King Loved in the Little Maid

BRAVE LITTLE SOLDIER—a soldier of Christ, someone who fights to become more like Jesus every day and bears his cross as Christ did

Chapter 15—How the King Found the Little Maid Sad One Day

PRINCESSES—female Christians striving to imitate Jesus so as to be crowned by Him in death

Chapter 16—The Golden City

OWN COUNTRY—our home in heaven

PALACE—that part of heaven, the new Jerusalem, where God sits upon the throne

A WORK TO DO—our growth in grace, sanctification, the use of our gifts to further the kingdom of God

LENS—the gift of faith

Chapter 17—The Land of Weary Waiting

LAND OF WEARY WAITING—Purgatory

Chapter 18—Brave Love

SAVE UP HER PENNIES—offer her merits and indulgences for the holy souls in Purgatory even at the cost of having none left for herself

Chapter 19—The King in His Beauty

TRAINING TO COME TO AN END—our Christian training which causes us to desire to be like Jesus and to please Him in all things—ends only with our death

COME IN YOUR DISGUISE TO THE LITTLE HUT—Jesus as plain Bread coming into our hearts in Holy Communion

Answer Key for the Matching Exercise on the Mass

Introductory Rites and Liturgy of the Word

"... in the name of the Father, and of the Son, and of the Holy Spirit."

"Amen."

"The Lord be with you."

"And with your spirit."

"I have greatly sinned . . ."

"... and in what I have failed to do . . ."

"Glory to God in the highest . . ."

"Lord Jesus Christ, Only Begotten Son . . ."

"You are seated at the right hand of the Father . . ."

"Thanks be to God . . ."

"Alleluia."

Scriptural Citation

2 Corinthians 9:15

Matthew 28:19

Luke 2:14

Galatians 6:18

Luke 1:28

James 4:17

Revelation 5:14

John 1:14

Revelation 19:1-7

1 Chronicles 21:8

Mark 16:19

Liturgy of the Eucharist and Concluding Rites

"Lift up your hearts."

"Holy, holy, holy . . ."

"While they were eating, he took bread . . . this is my body."

"When we eat this bread and drink this cup . . ."

"Our Father . . ."

"... as we await the blessed hope and the coming of our Savior . . ."

"Lamb of God, who takes away the sins of the world"

"Blessed is he who comes in the name of the Lord. Hosanna in the highest."

"Through him, with him, in him . . ."

"Peace be with you."

"Lord, I am not worthy to have you enter under my roof . . ."

Scriptural Citation

Lamentations 3:41 and Colossians 3:1-2

John 1:29

Isaiah 6:3

Matthew 8:8

Matthew 21:9

Titus 2:13

Matthew 6:9-13

Romans 11:36

1 Corinthians 11:26

Matthew 26:26-28

Luke 24:36 and Romans 15:33

Actions of the Mass

Sign of the Cross

Confessing Our Sins

Asking for God's Mercy

Homily (Explaining the Readings)

Intercessory Prayer (Praying for the Needs of Others)

Washing of the Hands

Being Sent Forth to Proclaim the Gospel

Scriptural Citation

Exodus 30:17-21

Psalm 51:1-4

Ezekiel 9:4-6

1 Timothy 2:1-4

Nehemiah 8:8 and Mark 1:21-22

James 5:16 and 1 Corinthians 11:27-28

John 20:21

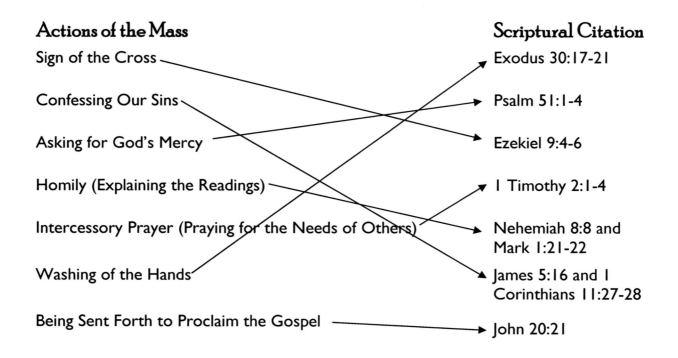

Bibliography

Anderson, Ken. *Where to Find It in the Bible*. Nashville, Tennessee: Thomas Nelson, Inc., 1996.

Aquilina, Mike and Regis J. Flaherty. *The How-To Book of Catholic Devotions*. Huntington, Indiana: Our Sunday Visitor Publishing Division, 2000.

Ball, Ann. *Modern Saints, Their Lives and Faces, Book Two*. Rockford, Illinois: Tan Books and Publishers, 1990.

Baudouin-Croix, Marie. *Léonie Martin: A Difficult Life*. Dublin, Ireland: Veritas Publications, 1993.

Clarke, John, O.C.D., Translator. *St. Thérese of Lisieux General Correspondence, Volume I, 1877-1890*. Washington, D.C.: Washington Province of Discalced Carmelites, Inc., 1982.

Coniker, Jerome F., Compiler. *Family Consecration Prayer & Meditation Book, Divine Mercy Edition*. Bloomingdale, Ohio: Apostolate for Family Consecration, 1998.

Guyot, Rev. G.H. *Scriptural References for the Baltimore Catechism, The Biblical Basis for Catholic Beliefs*. Harrison, New York: Roman Catholic Books, 1946.

Husslein, Rev. Joseph, S.J. *The Little Flower and the Blessed Sacrament*. New York, New York: Benziger Brothers, 1925.

Kinney, Donald, O.C.D., Translator. *The Poetry of St. Thérese of Lisieux*. Washington, D.C.: Institute of Carmelite Studies, 1996.

Kowalska, Sr. M. Faustina. *Divine Mercy in My Soul, The Diary of the Servant of God, Sr. M. Faustina Kowalska*. Stockbridge, Massachusetts: Marian Press, 1987.

Libreria Editrice Vaticana. *Catechism of the Catholic Church*. Washington, D.C.: United States Catholic Conference, Inc., Second Edition, 1997.

Lord, Daniel A., S.J. *Christ in Me*. Milwaukee, Wisconsin: Bruce Publishing Company, 1952.

Loyola, Mother Mary. *The King of the Golden City: An Allegory for Children*. New York: P.J. Kenedy & Sons, 1928.

Montessori, Maria. *The Mass Explained to Children*. Fort Collins, Colorado: Roman Catholic Books, originally published in 1932.

Mother Agnes of Jesus, O.C.D. *Little Counsels of Mother Agnes of Jesus, OCD*. Parnell, Michigan: Ideal Publishing Company, 1982.

Peers, Allison. Translator. *The Complete Works of St. John of the Cross*. Westminster, Maryland: The Newman Press: 1949. (The more modern translation by Kieran Kavanaugh, OCD, and Otilio Rodriguez, OCD is the recommended translation.)

Peers, Allison. Translator. *The Complete Works of St. Teresa of Jesus.* London and New York: Sheed & Ward, 1946. (The more modern translation by Kieran Kavanaugh, OCD, and Otilio Rodriguez, OCD is the recommended translation.)

Piat, Fr. Stéphane-Joseph, O.F.M. *Céline, Sr. Geneviéve of the Holy Face: Sister and Witness to St. Thérèse of the Child Jesus.* San Francisco, California: Ignatius Press, 1997.

Piat, Fr. Stéphane-Joseph, O.F.M. *The Story of a Family, The Home of St. Thérèse of Lisieux.* Rockford, Illinois: Tan Books and Publishers, 1994.

Roberto, Brother, C.S.C. *St. Therese Martin.* Notre Dame: Dujarie Press, 1967.

Rooney, Elizabeth. "Oblation." "Weavings." Vol. VII, No. 4 (July/August, 1992).

Ryan, Brother Ernest, C.S.C. *The Little Flower: A Story of St. Therese of the Child Jesus.* Notre Dame: Dujarie Press, 1959.

St. Thérèse of Lisieux. *The Story of a Soul, The Autobiography of St. Thérèse of Lisieux.* Rockford, Illinois: Tan Books and Publishers, 1997.

St. Thérèse of Lisieux. *Story of a Soul, The Autobiography of St. Thérèse of Lisieux.* Washington, D.C.: Institute of Carmelite Studies, 1976.

Sr. Mary Lucia of the Immaculate Heart. *Fatima in Lucia's Own Words, Sr. Lucia's Memoirs.* Fatima, Portugal: Postulation Centre, 1989.

Sri, Edward. *A Biblical Walk through the Mass: Understanding What We Say and Do in the Liturgy.* West Chester, Pennsylvania: Ascension Press, 2011.

Taylor, Thomas. Translator. *The Story of a Soul.* London: Burns, Oates & Washbourne, 1912. (The more modern translation by John Clarke is the recommended translation.)

Thompson, Blanche Jennings. *A Candle Burns for France.* Milwaukee: The Bruce Publishing Company: 1946.

Vaughan, Rev. Kenelm and Rev. Newton Thompson, S.T.D. *Scripture by Topic.* Fort Collins, Colorado: Roman Catholic Books, 1943.

Williams, Thomas David. *A Textual Concordance of the Holy Scriptures.* Rockford, Illinois: Tan Books and Publishers, 1985.

Windeatt, Mary Fabyan. *The Little Flower, The Story of St. Therese of the Child Jesus.* Rockford, Illinois: Tan Books and Publishers, 1991.

Windeatt, Mary Fabyan. *The Children of Fatima, and Our Lady's Message to the World.* Rockford, Illinois: Tan Books and Publishers, 1991.

Windeatt, Mary Fabyan. *The Patron Saint of First Communicants, The Story of Blessed Imelda Lambertini.* Rockford, Illinois: Tan Books and Publishers, 1991.

Other RACE for Heaven Products

Catholic Study Guides for Mary Fabyan Windeatt's Saint Biography Series:

RACE for Heaven study guides use the saint biographies of Mary Fabyan Windeatt to teach the Catholic faith to all members of your family. Written with your family's various learning levels in mind, these flexible study guides succeed as stand-alone unit studies or supplements to your regular curriculum. Thirty to sixty minutes per day will allow your family to experience:

- ☑ The spirituality and holy habits of the saints
- ☑ Lively family discussions on important faith topics
- ☑ Increased critical thinking and reading comprehension skills
- ☑ Quality read-aloud time with Catholic "living books"
- ☑ Enhanced knowledge of Catholic doctrine and the Bible
- ☑ History and geography incorporated into saintly literature
- ☑ Writing projects based on secular and Catholic historical events and characters

Purchase these guides individually or in the following grade-level packages. (Grades are determined solely on the length of each book in the series.)

Grades 3-4: *St. Thomas Aquinas, The Story of the "Dumb Ox"; St. Catherine of Siena, The Girl Who Saw Saints in the Sky; Patron Saint of First Communicants, The Story of Blessed Imelda Lambertini;* and *The Miraculous Medal, The Story of Our Lady's Appearances to St. Catherine Labouré*

Grade 5: *St. Rose, First Canonized Saint of the Americas; St. Martin de Porres, The Story of the Little Doctor of Lima, Peru; King David and His Songs, A Story of the Psalms;* and *Blessed Marie of New France, The Story of the First Missionary Sisters in Canada*

Grade 6: *St. Dominic, Preacher of the Rosary and Founder of the Dominicans; St. Benedict, The Story of the Father of the Western Monks; The Children of Fatima and Our Lady's Message to the World;* and *St. John Masias, Marvelous Dominican Gate-keeper of Lima, Peru*

Grade 7: *The Little Flower, The Story of St. Therese of the Child Jesus; St. Hyacinth, The Story of the Apostle of the North; The Curé of Ars, The Story of St. John Vianney, Patron Saint of Parish Priests;* and *St. Louis de Montfort, The Story of Our Lady's Slave*

Grade 8: *Pauline Jaricot, Foundress of the Living Rosary and the Society for the Propagation of Faith; St. Francis Solano, Wonder-Worker of the New World and Apostle of Argentina and Peru; St. Paul the Apostle, The Story of the Apostle to the Gentiles;* and *St. Margaret Mary, Apostle of the Sacred Heart*

The Windeatt Dictionary: Pre-Vatican II Terms and Catholic Words from Mary Fabyan Windeatt's Saint Biographies explains over 450 Catholic terms and expressions used in this popular saint biography series. Indispensable in expanding knowledge and practice of the Catholic faith, this book provides a ready access for the Catholic vocabulary words used in the RACE for Heaven Windeatt study guides. This dictionary also includes a Catholic book report resource that contains suggestions for forty-five Catholic book reports: fourteen writing projects, ten book report activities, and twenty-one topics for saint biographies.

Graced Encounters with Mary Fabyan Windeatt's Saints: 344 Ways to Imitate the Holy Habits of the Saints is a compilation of the "Growing in Holiness" sections of RACE for Heaven's Catholic study guides for the Windeatt saint biography series and presents 344 examples of saintly behavior, one for nearly every chapter in each of these twenty biographies. Enhance your encounter with the saints by practicing the models of devotion, service, penance, prayer, and virtue offered in this guide.

Bedtime Bible Stories for Catholic Children: Loving Jesus through His Word contains twenty discussions of Bible stories that were originally published in serial form in a Catholic children's magazine. Their author stated, "The tales are extremely simple and unadorned. They are real conversations of a real child and her mother." Due to popular demand, the series was later (1910) published as a book, *Bible Stories Told to "Toddles."* The engaging conversational style of this book lends itself well as a bedtime read-aloud that allows Jesus to come alive in the Gospels. The study aids include discussion questions to help foster spiritual conversation, Bible excerpts relevant to the presented story, "Growing in Holiness" suggestions for living the Gospel message in our daily lives, and short catechism lessons for both children and adults.

I Talk with God: The Art of Prayer and Meditation for Catholic Children strives to instill in young Catholics a love of prayer and a practical knowledge of the art of meditation. This prayer book contains prayers to pray out loud (vocal prayer) or in the silence of your heart. It shows how you can talk with God, and more importantly, how you can love God. As you progress through this book—from discovering what prayer is to reading and reciting simple prayers to understanding meditation and then to helps for deeper meditation—you will see that prayer and meditation often go together. Meditation is described by the big *Catechism of the Catholic Church* as nothing more than "prayerful reflection" or *holy thinking.* You can use books, devotions, pictures, holy cards, and images (such as the stained glass windows in church) to help you think about holy people, events, and ideas. Learn how to talk with God each day to increase your love for Him and follow more closely His holy will.

The King of the Golden City Study Edition is a new edition of a book that was originally published in 1921. This treasure of a book was written in response to a student's appeal for instructions along with "little stories" to help her prepare for Holy Communion. To fulfill this request, Mother Loyola of the Bar Convent in York, England, wrote a simple story that illustrates Jesus' desire to share an intimate relationship with each one of His children. This new edition contains some updated language but, quite deliberately, does not contain any pictures. Readers, as they progress through this story, will form a mental image of their King, one as unique and personal as their own relationship with Him. The study sections assist with the allegory, connect to the Bible as well as to the catechism, and explore the art of prayer in the spirit of the three Carmelite Doctors of the Church. Although written over ninety years ago for a young child, this book remains a timeless masterpiece of Catholic literature suitable for all ages. (Also available as a study guide only)

The Good Shepherd and His Little Lambs Study Edition is a simply told Catholic tale of four children who meet with their beloved aunt for "First Communion talks." More than a story, it is a First Communion primer that takes the tenets of the catechism and, through naturally-flowing conversations, relates them in the language of little ones to authentic Christian living. As Mrs. Bosch explains, "We might learn the catechism all the way through beautifully, and at the end find ourselves still very stiff and clumsy about loving our Lord. When He comes to us, we don't want to welcome Him into our souls only with answers out of the catechism, do we?" Enriched by appropriate Biblical passages, points of doctrine, and prayers, this story-primer is an enjoyable and effective read-aloud that will prepare the Good Shepherd's little lambs to worthily receive Him in the Holy Eucharist.

A Reconciliation Reader-Retreat: Read-Aloud Lessons, Stories, and Poems for Young Catholics Preparing for Confession provides a basic doctrinal explanation and review of the Sacrament of Reconciliation as well as a Gospel examination of conscience—a seven-day read-aloud formation retreat. To help the lessons come alive and to enable young Catholics to more readily apply these doctrines to their own daily lives, the lessons have been supplemented with pertinent short stories and poems. Each lesson contains reflection questions, a family prayer, and a "Gospel Examination of Conscience" that is formulated according to the dictates of the *Catechism of the Catholic Church*. This reader-retreat will not only enrich and deepen the sacramental experience for each member of your family but it will also provide several tools to help you recommit to leading a virtuous life and to grow together in holiness.

Devotion to St. Joseph: Read-Aloud Stories, Poems, and Prayers for Catholic Children encourages children to love Jesus as St. Joseph did. As Scripture does not record a single word this great saint spoke; we must take our lessons of his life from his actions. In this compilation of stories and poems about our Savior's foster-father from renowned Catholics, children of all ages are encouraged to imitate the virtues the life of St. Joseph reveal to us in his loving dedication to Jesus and Mary. The discussion questions as well as the reflections on the virtues of St. Joseph lead children to apply the lessons of this saint's life to their own while the prayer section promotes a lasting devotion to the great St. Joseph. As St. Teresa of Avila declared, "I wish I could persuade everyone to be devoted to this glorious saint!"

Alternative Book Reports for Catholic Students contains forty-five book report ideas to encourage critical thinking for ages seven to fourteen. These ideas are intended to provoke a reflection on those themes and topics that support and encourage Catholic living as well as some that may conflict with our Faith. Many report topics require an examination of our personal faith life and prompt us to take lessons from the saints to strengthen our own faith in God. The suggested activities vary from written exercises to creative art projects and include twenty-one topics specifically designed for saint biographies. Other activities can be used within a group or family.

Reading the Saints: Lists of Catholic Books for Children Plus Book Collecting Tips for the Home and School Library (formerly entitled *Saintly Resources*) is a valuable tool for Catholic home educators, classroom teachers, and collectors of Catholic juvenile books. This resource will help you discover living books from such popular out-of-print Catholic juvenile series as Catholic Treasury, Vision Books, and American Background Books as well as current series books for young Catholics. Use this book to find:

- Over 800 Catholic books listed by author, series, reading level, century, and geographical location

- More than 275 authors of saint biographies, historical fiction, and poetry written for Catholic juvenile readers

- Publishers of Catholic children's books, present and past

- Helpful advice for collecting and caring for used books

- Hundreds of age-appropriate, accessible living books to enrich your study of the Catholic Church's rich heritage of saints and notable Catholic historical figures

- Information on how to build and maintain your own library of Catholic juvenile books

- Inspiring quotations about book collecting, reading, and the love of books

The Outlaws of Ravenhurst Study Edition contains a classic story of the persecution of Scottish Catholics that was first written in 1923 and was revised and reprinted in 1950. This 2009 edition of Sr. M. Imelda Wallace's *Outlaws of Ravenhurst* contains the revised story of 1950 plus chapter-by-chapter aids to assist readers in assimilating the book's strong Catholic elements into their own lives. The study section focuses on critical thinking, integration of biblical teachings, and the study of the virtuous life to which Christ calls us as mature Catholics. With its emphasis on virtues (theological and moral plus the gifts and fruits of the Holy Spirit), the spiritual and corporal works of mercy, and the Beatitudes, *Outlaws of Ravenhurst Study Edition* is a fun and effective catechetical tool for Catholics preparing for the Sacrament of Confirmation. (Also available as a study guide only)

The Family that Overtook Christ Study Edition: The Story of the Family of St. Bernard of Clairvaux is an excellent read for young adults who are preparing to receive the Sacrament of Confirmation. In this exciting chronicle of the life of twelfth-century knights, we have an entire family of nine saints who lay before us their individual means of achieving intimate union with Christ. Learn with the Fontaines family how to supernaturalize the natural, develop a God-consciousness, and attain sanctity by being yourself. Perfect for high-school read-aloud (or adult study), this new study edition has over 250 footnotes for increased comprehension and provides discussion/meditation points to promote the art of spiritual conversation. The appendix lists formulas of Catholic doctrine that are essential for confirmands not only to know but also to incorporate into their own spiritual lives.

A Confirmation Reader-Retreat: Read-Aloud Lessons, Stories and Poems for Young Catholics utilizes chapters from two excellent out-of-print Catholic books for children (*I Belong to God, Great Truths in Simple Stories for Children and Lovers of Children* by Lillian Clark; and *Children's Retreats in Preparation for First Confession, First Holy Communion, and Confirmation* by Rev. P.A. Halpin). This book provides a basic doctrinal review of the Sacrament of Confirmation as well as prayer experiences—a nine-day read-aloud retreat/novena. The reprinted material has been supplemented with short stories and poems that provide insights in applying catechetical doctrines to the daily life of young Catholics. Each lesson concludes with "I Talk with God"—a section that encourages readers (of all ages) to deepen their relationship with each of the Three Persons of the Blessed Trinity. Reflection questions promote the habit of spiritual conversation within your family—to encourage family members to discuss holy topics—and to help you grow together in holiness. Additionally, a traditional novena to the Holy Spirit is included.

To Order: Email info@RACEforHeaven.com or place an order at RACEforHeaven.com. Discover, MasterCard, VISA, PayPal, American Express, checks, and money orders are accepted.

CPSIA information can be obtained at www.ICGtesting.com
Printed in the USA
BVOW052246140512

290213BV00003B/2/P